4/96

MADONNA

★ ★ ★ ★ ★ ★ ★ ★ ★ ★ ★ ★

D0732378

POP CULTURE LEGENDS

MADONNA

★ ★ ★ ★ ★ ★ ★ ★ ★ ★ ★ ★ ★ ★ ★ ★ ★

NICOLE CLARO

CHELSEA HOUSE PUBLISHERS

New York ★ Philadelphia

CHELSEA HOUSE PUBLISHERS

EDITORIAL DIRECTOR   Richard Rennert
EXECUTIVE MANAGING EDITOR   Karyn Gullen Browne
COPY CHIEF   Robin James
PICTURE EDITOR   Adrian G. Allen
ART DIRECTOR   Robert Mitchell
MANUFACTURING DIRECTOR   Gerald Levine

Pop Culture Legends

SENIOR EDITOR   Kathy Kuhtz Campbell
SERIES DESIGN   Basia Niemczyc

Staff for MADONNA

ASSOCIATE EDITOR   Martin Schwabacher
EDITORIAL ASSISTANT   Kelsey Goss
PICTURE RESEARCHER   Wendy P. Wills
COVER ILLUSTRATION   Alan Reingold

Copyright © 1994 by Chelsea House Publishers, a division of
Main Line Book Co. All rights reserved. Printed and bound in the
United States of America.

3 5 7 9 8 6 4 2

Library of Congress Cataloging-in-Publication Data

Claro, Nicole.
Madonna/Nicole Claro.
p. cm.—(Pop culture legends)
Includes bibliographical references and index.
ISBN 0-7910-2330-3.
        0-7910-2355-9 (pbk.)
1. Madonna, 1959– —Juvenile literature. 2. Rock musicians—
United States—Biography—Juvenile literature. [1. Madonna,
1959– . 2. Musicians. 3. Women—Biography. 4. Rock music.] I.
Title. II. Series.
ML3930.M26C6 1994   93-30227
782.42166'092—dc20   CIP
[B]   AC MN

FRONTISPIECE:
An uncharacteristically subdued Madonna assumes an
introspective pose.

921
MADONNA
1994

Contents ★

A Reflection of Ourselves

Leeza Gibbons

I ENJOY A RARE PERSPECTIVE on the entertainment industry. From my window on popular culture, I can see all that sizzles and excites. I have interviewed legends who have left us, such as Bette Davis and Sammy Davis, Jr., and have brushed shoulders with the names who have caused a commotion with their sheer outrageousness, like Boy George and Madonna. Whether it's by nature or by design, pop icons generate interest, and I think they are a mirror of who we are at any given time.

Who are *your* heroes and heroines, the people you most admire? Outside of your own family and friends, to whom do you look for inspiration and guidance, as examples of the type of person you would like to be as an adult? How do we decide who will be the most popular and influential members of our society?

You may be surprised by your answers. According to recent polls, you will probably respond much differently than your parents or grandparents did to the same questions at the same age. Increasingly, world leaders such as Winston Churchill, John F. Kennedy, Franklin D. Roosevelt, and evangelist Billy Graham have been replaced by entertainers, athletes, and popular artists as the individuals whom young people most respect and admire. In surveys taken during each of the past 15 years, for example, General Norman Schwarzkopf was the only world leader chosen as the number-one hero among high school students. Other names on the elite list joined by General Schwarzkopf included Paula Abdul, Michael Jackson, Michael Jordan, Eddie Murphy, Burt Reynolds, and Sylvester Stallone.

More than 30 years have passed since Canadian sociologist Marshall McLuhan first taught us the huge impact that the electronic media has had on how we think, learn, and understand—as well as how we choose our heroes. In the 1960s, Pop artist Andy Warhol predicted that there would soon come a time when every American would be famous for 15 minutes. But if it is easier today to achieve Warhol's 15 minutes of fame, it is also much harder to hold on to it. Reputations are often ruined as quickly as they are made.

And yet, there remain those artists and performers who continue to inspire and instruct us in spite of changes in world events, media technology, or popular tastes. Even in a society as fickle and fast moving as our own, there are still those performers whose work and reputation endure, pop culture legends who inspire an almost religious devotion from their fans.

Why do the works and personalities of some artists continue to fascinate us while others are so quickly forgotten? What, if any, qualities do they share that enable them to have such power over our lives? There are no easy answers to these questions. The artists and entertainers profiled in this series often have little more in common than the enormous influence that each of them has had on our lives.

Some offer us an escape. Artists such as actress Marilyn Monroe, comedian Groucho Marx, and writer Stephen King have used glamour, humor, or fantasy to help us escape from our everyday lives. Others present us with images that are all too recognizable. The uncompromising realism of actor and director Charlie Chaplin and folk singer Bob Dylan challenges us to confront and change the things in our world that most disturb us.

Some offer us friendly, reassuring experiences. The work of animator Walt Disney and late-night talk show host Johnny Carson, for example, provides us with a sense of security and continuity in a changing world. Others shake us up. The best work of composer John Lennon and actor James Dean will always inspire their fans to question and reevaluate the world in which they live.

It is also hard to predict the kind of life that a pop culture legend will lead, or how he or she will react to fame. Popular singers Michael Jackson

and Prince carefully guard their personal lives from public view. Other performers, such as popular singer Madonna, enjoy putting their private lives before the public eye.

What these artists and entertainers do share, however, is the rare ability to capture and hold the public's imagination in a world dominated by mass media and disposable celebrity. In spite of their differences, each of them has somehow managed to achieve legendary status in a popular culture that values novelty and change.

The books in this series examine the lives and careers of these and other pop culture legends, and the society that places such great value on their work. Each book considers the extraordinary talent, the stubborn commitment, and the great personal sacrifice required to create work of enduring quality and influence in today's world.

As you read these books, ask yourself the following questions: How are the careers of these individuals shaped by their society? What role do they play in shaping the world? And what is it that so captivates us about their lives, their work, or the images they present?

Hopefully, by studying the lives and achievements of these pop culture legends, we will learn more about ourselves.

Blonde Ambition

HEAVY WIND BATTERED the area around the outdoor arena. The determined performer stood defiantly at the center of the giant stage. A special microphone was clipped to her coiffed blond hair, and a song was booming out of her taut, diminutive frame. Millions of people all over the world knew her voice, her face, her body, and all the various guises she had worn since she had taken the pop music world by storm nearly 10 years earlier. Famous for her tenacity and strong will, Madonna knew the show must go on.

In another minute, the stage would be slicked with rain, making it more like an ice-skating rink than the elegant floor needed to accommodate dancers, singers, musicians, and a series of lavish stage sets. The crew of one of the most controversial tours in the history of pop music worked feverishly, its members praying they could use their Hollywood magic to battle the storm.

It was Friday, May 13, 1990, the opening day of Madonna's new tour. Months of preparation and millions of dollars had gone into planning what Madonna hoped would be the most daring and exciting concert tour in

Madonna strikes a commanding pose during her 1990 Blonde Ambition tour.

history. The site chosen to launch the tour was Chiba, a suburb of Tokyo, Japan. Unfortunately, no one had taken into account that the first show had been scheduled to occur during the height of Japan's rainy season.

With the wind swirling about them, Madonna and her dancers continued to rehearse the show. Though it was not yet raining, menacing clouds had gathered, and it was clearly only a matter of time before those clouds unleashed a raging storm. The tour's technicians had good reason to be concerned about mechanical mishaps. Three times during rehearsals in Los Angeles, a trapdoor in the center of the stage (intended for set changes) had flown open while Madonna was standing precariously nearby.

Mechanical glitches were easily overcome; the weather, however, was a different matter. While the Tokyo clouds hovered, threatening to let loose at any moment, Madonna stood firm on the huge stage, giving orders and working through each number. She sang and danced, acknowledging the weather but never letting it get the best of her.

What possessed this woman to insist, with fierce determination, that a show of this scale could be mounted against the ancient force of a Japanese rainstorm? One factor impossible to ignore was that 35,000 fans had paid more than $1.5 million for tickets to the show. On one of Madonna's previous tours in Japan, bad weather had forced her to cancel a concert. A near riot had ensued. If Madonna canceled this performance, her tight schedule would make it impossible

Talk of Madonna's eye-popping outfits, designed by Jean-Paul Gaultier, preceded her as she took her blockbuster show around the world in 1990.

to rebook the show. There was no telling what chaos might result if the thousands of fans who had braved the weather to come to the stadium were denied the chance to see her. Besides, her proud, competitive nature would not allow her to quit when there were so many people in the audience who were more than willing to endure the rain. As Madonna told *People* magazine, "When I saw the kids in front getting soaked, the decision was made."

More than anything else, however, it was simply her nature to push on in situations such as this. Madonna had persevered in the face of adversity more than once in her life. Her mother died when Madonna was six years old, an event that had a powerful influence on her life and work. When she moved to New York City at the age of 19, she weathered hunger, lack of money, and near homelessness while struggling to establish herself. She had been her own best friend and had fought to make people hear her, see her, and notice her. She had made it to the top on her own steam. And she was not going to let a little rain stop her now.

Simultaneous with the first strains of "Express Yourself," Madonna's anthem to autonomy, the rain began to soak the stage. With her blond ponytail swinging and her ivory-colored corset shimmering in the lights, Madonna stepped out onto the already drenched stage and yelled "*Genki desu ka?*—How ya doin'?" to the eager audience. Thirty-five thousand Japanese fans, many of them teenage girls dressed in the various styles of their singing idol, screamed and danced as Madonna tore into the 18-song, 108-minute show. The language barrier did not seem to be an obstacle for Madonna or for her Japanese fans. She had, after all, performed throughout the world, entertaining people who might never have uttered a word of English. Madonna sang, danced, and joked, mesmerizing her audience and defeating nature itself, a force tougher than the harshest audience or critic.

This was her third and, perhaps, her most important tour. Each had outdone the previous one in musical and visual splendor. Madonna's medium was no longer just music; it was theater as well. On a raucous, glittery evening, this extravagant concert would truly bring those two worlds together. Competing against superstars like Michael Jackson and Prince, both known for their lavish stage shows, Madonna and her creative team were determined that this production would be a mind-blower. The show's choreographer, Vince Paterson, told *People* magazine that Madonna had wanted to "break every rule we can" and "change the shape of concerts." According to Paterson, Madonna said she "wanted to combine fashion, Broadway, rock and performance art."

The spectacle involved a full band, a troupe of male dancers, and two female backup singer/dancers, all in elaborate costumes designed by Jean-Paul Gaultier. Gaultier's gender-crossing creations for the show would spark a whole new style of dress—imitations of his bold new ideas would soon be cropping up all over the high fashion world. The show began with Madonna in a satin corset, the straps hanging down over men's trousers. Her female backup dancers were dressed similarly, while the men began the show shirtless, with rough work pants draped around their hips. Madonna would change costume—and persona—numerous times throughout the show, assuming with each transformation roles ranging from sweet schoolgirl to tough businesswoman to guises more racy and risqué. In the midst of the dazzling show of lights and bodies (dreamed up by Madonna's brother and art director, Christopher Ciccone), set pieces, including freestanding stairs and an altar flickering with numerous candles, would roll on and off the stage.

Because of the suggestive and provocative nature of much of the concert material, the Blonde Ambition tour was one of the most controversial live works Madonna

In a characteristic gender role switch, Madonna performed her hit song "Cherish" with male dancers dressed as half-human, half-fish mermen.

had ever attempted. In more than one city around the world, local authorities tried to block the show. In Rome, Italy, because of Vatican protests, ticket sales were so low that one of Madonna's two performances had to be canceled.

By breaking social and sexual barriers and taboos, Madonna has made herself a topic of debate, not only for her fans but for writers, news commentators, parents, academics, and aspiring artistes of all sorts. In short, Madonna is a pop culture icon for the 1980s and 1990s—and she is likely to remain popular into the next century. It is impossible to describe pop culture today without mentioning her name.

Madonna has kept her fans in suspense from the moment she burst onto the scene in 1983, searching for new looks, new sounds, and new artistic pursuits. She started out as a pop singer with a largely female, teenage audience. She had always wanted to act, however, and a parallel career in film was not far behind. As she broadened her artistic horizons, she drew fans of all types. She was one of the pioneer "video artists" of the new MTV generation, and she used the network to showcase her various transformations and escapades.

In some ways, her story is the stuff of which dreams are made. In other ways, it is a tale of hard work, tough times, and striving to earn the "big break." Madonna has been many things: a figure of controversy and of adulation, a sex symbol, a shrewd businesswoman, and, of course, a dancer, singer, and actress.

The Blonde Ambition tour, as it came to be known, was immortalized in the film *Truth or Dare,* which contains backstage, personal, and up-close moments the likes of which Madonna fans had never before seen. In *Truth or Dare,* just before she steps onstage for the rain-soaked show in Chiba, Madonna is seen telling her dancers that their costumes for the night will include their heavy tour jackets. Other than that, the show would go on exactly as planned.

After the show's triumphant conclusion, the star looks into the camera and says, "It was scary, but we did it." Despite the awful weather, the Chiba show did, indeed, go on. As her brother Christopher said, "She overcame rain, a full moon, and Friday the 13th, and put on a terrific show." It would not be the last storm she would have to face down through sheer force of will. Throughout her career, Madonna would do her best to stir up storms of controversy and protest. But always she would emerge victorious, the very model of a strong, independent woman eager to take on the world.

2 ☆ A Faded Smile

TO FIND THE EARLIEST SEEDS of Madonna's fierce ambition and determination to succeed, one has to look no further than the lives of her parents, Tony and Madonna Ciccone. Both were spirited, intelligent people who were not afraid to go after what they wanted—traits Madonna certainly inherited.

Tony Ciccone's background was similar to that of many second-generation immigrants. On June 2, 1931, he was born Silvio Ciccone to Italian immigrant parents in Pennsylvania. Gaetano and Michelina Ciccone had left the Italian village of Pacentro in 1928, looking for better opportunities in America. They settled in the largely Italian-American Pittsburgh suburb of Aliquippa, where Gaetano found work in the steel mills. As young Silvio grew up in the rough-and-tumble neighborhood, he eventually adopted the more American-sounding moniker "Tony." The youngest of the six Ciccone children, Tony was also the only one who would go on to college. He was ambitious, intelligent, fluent in both Italian and English, and strikingly handsome.

A rarely reproduced photograph from the West Middle School yearbook shows Madonna in the eighth grade.

ALBUQUERQUE ACADEMY
LIBRARY

The Jones and Laughlin Steel Corporation is one of many steel mills in Pittsburgh, Pennsylvania. Madonna's grandparents, Gaetano and Michelina Ciccone, left Italy in 1928 and came to Pittsburgh, where Gaetano found work in a steel mill. Madonna's father, Silvio, later called Tony, was born in Pittsburgh in 1931.

After college, armed with an engineering degree, Tony arrived in Michigan hoping to start a career in the booming automobile industry. He succeeded, landing a job as an optic and defense engineer with the Chrysler Corporation, where he worked on government weapons contracts at the company's missile and tank plant in Warren, Michigan. Eventually, in order to fulfill his military service, he joined the Air Force Reserves.

In the early 1950s, Tony Ciccone, then stationed in Texas with the Reserves, attended the wedding of his friend and fellow serviceman, Dale Fortin. Ciccone was finishing his military duty, which had begun with a stint in Alaska, before returning to Michigan and his engineering job. There, he met Fortin's younger sister, a beguiling, dark-haired beauty of French-Canadian descent. The spark was lit. Within a week, Madonna Louise Fortin broke off with the man to whom she was already engaged. In 1955, at Visitation Church in Bay City, Michigan, she and Tony were married.

Tony and Madonna began their life together in Pontiac, Michigan, a small town about 25 miles northwest of Detroit. In 1956, Madonna gave birth to their first son, Anthony. The following year another son, Martin, was born. On August 16, 1958, the young mother gave birth to her first girl. They named her Madonna Louise, but called her Little Nonni to distinguish her from her mother.

Madonna Fortin Ciccone was remarkable for her time. In the mid-1950s, most mothers stayed at home to raise their children. Madonna Ciccone worked full-time as an X-ray technician, in addition to cooking, cleaning, and caring for her family. "I remember her as being a very forgiving, angelic person," the younger Madonna has said. "She did all the housecleaning, and she was always picking up after us. We were really messy, awful kids."

By the end of the 1950s, the Ciccone clan was growing at a rapid pace. Paula Ciccone was born a year after Madonna. In 1960, Christopher arrived, followed by Melanie in 1962. Madonna and her siblings enjoyed a loving upbringing. Young Madonna herself was an outspoken, emotional toddler, and her brothers Anthony and Martin were no strangers to mischief. Yet even when they threw rocks at neighbors' windows or started fires in their own basement, their parents reacted with temperance. Tony and Madonna Ciccone never responded by yelling or screaming; according to Madonna, her parents "would just hug us and put their arms around us and talk to us quietly."

This did not mean that Madonna's parents did not have high standards—in fact, Madonna remembers her upbringing as quite strict and full of rules. But instead of punishing his children, Tony Ciccone led by example. "My father was very strong," recalled Madonna. "He did have integrity, and if he told us not to do something, he didn't do it either."

The influence of Catholicism was omnipresent in the Ciccone family. Both Tony and Madonna Ciccone had been raised devout Catholics and were determined to instill in their children the same respect for religion. "We used to get up every morning at six or seven and go to church for an hour before school," the singer recalled in a 1989 interview. Madonna herself attended Catholic schools through junior high. For a brief period, she even wanted to become a nun. To her, the sisters she had encountered at church and in school, in their elegant long habits, "were the most superhuman, and fabulous people." The rosary beads and crucifixes that Madonna later made into fashion statements were more than mere accessories. In fact, one of her most treasured possessions was a turquoise crucifix her grandmother had given her. This crucifix was so dear to her that, no matter what she was wearing, it was always around her neck.

The Ciccones' firm religious faith and love for one another could not protect them, however, from a tragedy that would alter their lives forever. During the summer

Madonna's childhood hometown of Pontiac, Michigan, just 25 miles from Detroit, was the site of many automobile factories, including those of the Chrysler corporation, where her father worked as an engineer.

that she was pregnant with Melanie, Madonna Ciccone developed breast cancer. Madonna, barely four years old at the time, quite clearly remembers the effects of her mother's illness on the family. As they were only young-sters, unable to understand the extent of their mother's condition, the children "wanted her to play with us. We wanted her to do things when she was tired; we picked on her all the time because we just didn't understand." Yet, she recalled, even in the face of this, her mother "never allowed herself any sort of self-pity . . . [or] to wallow in the tragedy of her situation. So in that respect I think she gave me an incredible lesson."

In 1987, Madonna told *American Film* magazine, "That period when I knew that my mother wasn't fulfill-ing her role—and realizing that I was losing her—has a lot to do with my fuel, so to speak, my fuel for life. It left me with an intense longing to fill a sort of emptiness." After spending a final year in the hospital, Madonna Ciccone died on December 1, 1963. She was 30 years old. Reflecting on the loss of her mother at such an early age, Madonna observed, "My mother's death left me with a certain kind of loneliness, an incredible longing for something. If I hadn't had that emptiness, I wouldn't have been so driven."

Madonna and her father had always been close. After her mother died, their bond became tighter than ever. "I knew how to wrap him around my finger," she claimed. "I knew there was another way to go besides saying, 'No, I'm not going to do it,' and I employed those tech-niques." According to Madonna, "I flirted with every-one—my uncles, my grandfather, my father, everybody. I was always aware of my female charm." She has even admitted, "I used to try to copy Shirley Temple when I was a little girl."

Madonna says she did not feel close to her siblings when she was growing up, and that she felt "like an outsider" in her house. Driven by this sense of isolation and the competition siblings in a large family often experience, she became a straight-A student in an attempt to win her father's approval. As incentive, the Ciccone children earned 50 cents for every A they brought home. "I got the most quarters," the always-competitive Madonna remembered.

Following her mother's death, Madonna took on as much of a maternal role as was possible for a six-year-old. Because she was the oldest girl, she did what she could to help raise her brothers and sisters. But she was motivated by more than a sense of responsibility. By attempting to fill her mother's role, she was also trying to take the privileged place her mother had held in her father's affections and claim her father for herself.

Several prospective housekeepers employed by their father could not deal with the six young Ciccone children. But, in 1966, three years after the death of Madonna's mother, Joan Gustafson came to take care of the children and the housework. Six months later, Tony Ciccone married her. The transition was not easy for Madonna. She felt that her stepmother threatened the insular, focused connection she and her father had formed. As Madonna puts it, "I lost my mother, but then I was the mother; my father was mine. Then he got taken away from me when he married my stepmother."

Madonna later realized how difficult it must have been for Joan Gustafson, still quite young herself, to inherit such a large family. But, she says, "I didn't resent having to raise my brothers and sisters as much as I resented the fact that I didn't have my mother. And that my ideal of my family was interrupted." Feeling that she and her stepmother were competing for her father's attention, Madonna resented her father's new wife and refused to accept her. "My father made us all call her Mom," she said, but "I couldn't, I wouldn't say it."

Madonna responded to the disruptions in her life with a marked change in her own behavior. She became more reserved and kept to herself. "It was then that I said, okay, I don't need anybody," she remembered. "No one's going to break my heart again. I'm not going to need anybody. I can stand on my own and be my own person and not belong to anyone."

But Madonna's resolve to be independent could not eliminate her need for attention, particularly from her father. She soon found new ways to get his attention while simultaneously asserting her defiance of him. The combination of a demand to be noticed with a fearless disregard for what others might think of her would become a central element of her future stage persona.

One of Madonna's first public performances came at the age of 10 during the talent show at St. Andrew's grammar school. St. Andrew's was located in Rochester, Michigan, the upscale, rather affluent neighborhood to which the Ciccone family had moved in the mid-1960s. Rochester was a classic American suburban neighborhood—clean, crime-free, with large yards for the numerous neighborhood kids to play in.

Even as a child, Madonna felt the need to stand out. "I always thought I should be treated like a star when I was a kid. The biggest piece of the cake," Madonna recalled. At school, Madonna reluctantly wore the same uniform that all the other girls wore. At home, she battled her stepmother over the homemade dresses that were identical to her sisters', altering the look with a bow in her hair or a brightly colored sweater. More than just assertions of her identity and independence, her acts of rebellion were also attempts to gain attention from the person she needed to notice her most—her father.

Tony Ciccone certainly noticed when his 10-year-old daughter woke up the audience at the St. Andrew's talent show by launching into a go-go dance routine, but he was

not at all pleased with what he saw. To the strains of
"Baba O'Reilly" by the Who, Madonna came spinning
onto the stage dressed only in a bikini and body paint,
making it look as if she were completely nude. Although
she received a huge ovation, Madonna was grounded for
two weeks afterward by her outraged father. The young
exhibitionist was unrepentant. "I *was* practically naked,"
she admitted years later, "but the talent show was my
one night a year to show them who I really was and what
I could really be, and I just wanted to do totally outrageous stuff."

St. Andrew's was only the beginning for the budding
performer. When she was 13, she appeared in her first
film, in which neighborhood friends pretended to fry an
egg on her bare stomach. In the midst of this early
experimentation, Madonna remained a straight-A student. She was involved in many school activities and
still went to church regularly. But, by early adolescence,
Madonna began to question her father regarding the rules
and regulations of such things as organized prayer and
the proper dress for Mass. Madonna later remembered
"being really annoyed that I couldn't wear pants to
school or church. My brother could, and that seemed to
me all locked up with the religion. I kept saying to my
father, 'But why can't I love God the same way if I have
pants on?'"

Madonna has described this period of her childhood
as the beginning of a series of small rebellions. Though
she was in awe of the sisters who were teaching her in
grade school, they often scolded or punished her. Even
now, Madonna sparks much controversy over her "good
girl/bad girl" image, a poignant combination of proper
Catholic girlhood and furious rebellion. Most observers
notice only her willful defiance and urge to shock, but the
roots of Catholic discipline run equally deep in her
psyche. At West Junior High, her first public school, she

was a straight-A student, faithfully attending Mass every day before school and confessing regularly. At her church confirmation in 1966, she chose the name Veronica to add to her given name. According to Madonna, Saint Veronica was a woman who "wiped the face of Jesus and then carried around the cloth with his blood and sweat on it," an image that fascinated her.

By the time she reached junior high, Madonna had also discovered boys. She knew her habit of chasing the boys in the school yard caused discomfort to both the nuns and her father. "I wanted to chase after boys, and the nuns told me I couldn't, that good Catholic girls didn't chase boys," she remembers. "I didn't understand what was so bad about it, so I would do it anyway." Once, when she was in the fourth grade, she tore off her shirt and flung herself at a little boy named Tommy. Her assertiveness was rewarded with her first kiss.

Madonna has spoken about her father's belief that one should never be idle and that every waking moment should be productive. Tony Ciccone insisted that each of his children choose a musical instrument and practice it every day. Madonna had a brief flirtation with piano lessons, but they did not hold her interest. Finally, she convinced her father to let her enroll instead at a local dance studio. She later described it as "one of those places where you get ballet, jazz, tap, and baton twirling." But for Madonna, who loved to dance even as a small child,

Madonna, shown here in her freshman yearbook photograph, was always active in the arts. At Rochester Adams High School, she started a drama club, the Thespians, and starred in several productions.

27

lessons offered a true opportunity to express herself. When she was younger she had loved to teach the other children to dance to her pop music records, and later, at school dances, her wild, unrestrained gyrations would arouse awe in her classmates.

In 1971, Madonna spent the summer between her eighth and ninth grades in Bay City at her maternal grandmother Elsie Fortin's house. Madonna's grandmother was quite a bit more lenient than Tony and Joan Ciccone. The teenage Madonna was allowed to wear makeup and stay out late to watch her uncles' band play at local bars and clubs. It was her first exposure to the world of live music, and she loved it. According to Madonna, she thought at the time, "Yeah, this is it, I'm *cool!*"

In 1972, Madonna entered Rochester Adams High School, where she joined the cheerleading squad and the French club and sang in the school choir. She also founded the Thespians, the school drama club. That same year, Madonna made a step up in her pursuit of dance, enrolling at Christopher Flynn's ballet school in Detroit. It would be her entry into a whole new world.

In an interview excerpted in Christopher Andersen's book *Madonna: Unauthorized,* Flynn recalled his first impressions of Madonna. He vividly remembered that she often brought with her to class a girl doll, almost half as tall as she was, with a little dress. Madonna looked, he said, "like the most innocent girl in the world."

Madonna and Flynn formed an intense bond right away. He encouraged her not only artistically but emotionally as well. One day after class, as Madonna stood gazing out the studio window, Flynn came up behind her and said, "God, you're really beautiful." To her amazement, he continued, "You have an ancient-looking face. A face like an ancient Roman statue."

Madonna has more than once called that moment a turning point in her life, because she was then "fourteen

Madonna seizes center stage in her ninth grade yearbook cheerleading photo.

and feeling horribly unattractive and unpopular and un-interesting and unfabulous." She credits Flynn with tak-ing her out of what she considered to be her "humdrum existence."

Madonna worked hard at her dancing, especially be-cause she was one of Flynn's youngest students. She and Flynn became closer. At 16, she began accompanying him to Detroit's gay discos, where she let loose on the dance floor, and her future persona began to emerge. Sur-rounded by gay men, Madonna was often the only woman on the floor, but she felt right at home. The men loved her audacious dancing, and were amused when she would jokingly flirt with them, sometimes dancing with two men at a time. She became a crowd favorite.

Meanwhile, she remained a straight-A student at school. She was still participating in school productions, starring in performances of *My Fair Lady, The Wizard of Oz, Godspell,* and *Cinderella* with the drama club she had formed. But the bubbly, outgoing girl was becoming a bit more introverted and serious. By her junior year, she had quit the cheerleading squad. She became a vegetarian and, no longer under the constraints of a school uniform, began dressing to please herself. Her new mode of fashion included baggy pants that were ripped all over and held together with safety pins—a look influenced by the "punk rock" movement sweeping cities all across the country in the mid-1970s.

Madonna became more and more immersed in her dancing and in her relationship with Christopher Flynn. Keenly aware of Madonna's potential, Flynn felt she needed a more diverse atmosphere in which to explore her creative gifts. At his urging, she applied to the arts program at the University of Michigan, where Flynn had just accepted a job in the dance department. Madonna received a glowing recommendation from her Russian history teacher, Marilyn Fallows, who called her "an intelligent, sensitive, and creative young woman." Her guidance counselor, Nancy Ryan Mitchell, characterized Madonna in her own letter as "dynamic, vivacious, truly alive," with a "sparkling personality." These recommendations, Madonna's impeccable academic record, and her potential as a dancer made her a prime candidate for a scholarship to the university, an honor she indeed won.

Madonna's success came as no surprise to Mitchell, who said in *Madonna: Unauthorized,* "Even then, those of us on the faculty were sort of in awe of her." According-

As a senior in high school, Madonna earned straight A's and impressed her teachers with her drive and independence.

ing to the guidance counselor, Madonna had needed very little guidance, and, in fact, "never asked our opinion about anything. Madonna always knew exactly what she wanted, and how to get it. Usually, she'd come to me to sign authorization slips. I can still see her come breezing into my office, chewing gum frantically. She'd slap a form on my desk—completely filled out—and say, 'Hey, I need you to sign this application for me.' Not rude—she'd always thank me—but very direct."

It is interesting to note that three of the shows in which Madonna appeared in high school—*My Fair Lady, The Wizard of Oz,* and *Cinderella*—all concern young women who are transported from their humdrum existences into magical lives filled with beauty and excitement. As the star and founder of the drama club, Madonna probably played a leading role in selecting the group's material, and these stories may have appealed to her own personal fantasies. Of course, these plays have achieved popularity because they appeal to dreams shared by almost everybody. For Madonna, however, graduation from high school meant it was time to start turning her dreams into reality.

3 Who's That Girl?

IN THE FALL OF 1976, Madonna packed her bags, said good-bye to her family, and left for Ann Arbor, Michigan, to study modern dance. The University of Michigan had a well-respected arts program, and Madonna took classes in dance, music, and art. Madonna kept to herself while she was there, and, she says, made a point of standing apart from the other dancers. In 1984, she told *Rolling Stone*, "I was a real ham. I did everything I could to get attention and be the opposite of everyone else. I'd rip my leotards and wear teeny little safety pins. And I'd run my tights. I could have gone to a nightclub right after class."

Her behavior did not win her many friends among the other dance students, and she began spending time alone in the clubs and bars of the university town. In one of these, the Blue Frogge, a local pub frequented by college students, she met Steve Bray, a tall, handsome musician who played drums in a rhythm and blues group. Madonna was drawn to him—"First guy I ever asked to buy me a drink," she quipped later—and began seeing him romantically. Steve Bray, overwhelmed by the feisty, ebullient dance

---

Internationally renowned modern dancer and choreographer Pearl Lang was Madonna's first mentor in New York City.

Madonna spent just one and a half years on the pleasant midwestern campus of the University of Michigan before bolting to New York City in 1978.

student, later said, "She stood out, quite. Her energy was really apparent." Madonna often accompanied Bray to his shows, dancing with a girlfriend while his band played.

Even with the diversion of Bray's band, Madonna soon became restless in the university atmosphere, which was, for her, too structured. Christopher Flynn, who was teaching at the university, encouraged her to follow her instincts and move to New York. "Stop wasting your time in the sticks," he told her. "Take your little behind to New York. Go!" After only a year and a half in college, Madonna decided to drop out of school and try to make it as a dancer.

With only $35 in her pocket and no blessing from her father, Madonna left Michigan and headed for New York City. In July 1978, she stepped off the plane and into a taxicab, where she told the driver, "Take me to the center of everything." The next thing she knew, she was in the middle of the seedy turmoil of Times Square, hardly a place for a midwestern girl new to the teeming, noisy streets of New York City. In addition, the cab ride had cost her about half of the little money she had with her. Almost immediately, though, the resourceful Madonna met a kind stranger who took her in until she found a place of her own.

Such was the pattern of Madonna's "getting by" in the Big Apple. Until her first management deal, which would not take place for another three years, Madonna hopped from one friend's apartment to another, squatting in abandoned buildings when she could, and later living in her music studio. Often hungry, Madonna was at times forced to scavenge food from garbage cans.

Madonna was not so concerned with her living arrangements as she was with pursuing her dance career in New York. Almost as soon as she arrived there, Christopher Flynn, still her creative mentor, encouraged Madonna to apply for a scholarship to the American Dance Festival (ADF), held over a six-week period each summer at Duke University in Durham, North Carolina. Pearl Lang, an internationally known dancer and choreographer, whom Madonna had seen perform at the University of Michigan, was teaching an ADF workshop that year. Lang had been the lead soloist for Martha Graham's renowned modern dance company and had cofounded the American Dance Center in New York with choreographer Alvin Ailey.

In order to attend the workshop, however, Madonna had to win one of only six scholarships available to 600 applicants. When it was her turn to audition, Lang remembered, "Madonna walked right up to the table and looked straight at me and declared, 'I'm auditioning for this scholarship so I can work with Pearl Lang. I've seen one of her performances and she's the only one I want to work with.'" When Lang revealed who she was, she recalled, "Madonna's eyes popped out of her head."

Madonna went on to win a scholarship with her audition, but in the opinion of one classmate, Madonna's performance really began with her introduction to Lang. "Pearl Lang was pointed out to her before the audition," the student recalled. "Madonna knew *exactly* who she was talking to. Corny, but it worked."

When she returned to New York in late July, Madonna took more classes at the American Dance Center, but she found the competition overwhelming. She would often end up sitting by the fountain at Lincoln Center, crying.

One of Madonna's heroes while she was pursuing a career in dance was choreographer Martha Graham (shown here in 1940). Graham's intense, visceral, angular style of movement rejected the graceful artifice of ballet and exerted a defining influence on the development of modern dance. A long-standing dream of Madonna's is to star in a movie version of Graham's life.

"I'd write in my journal," she told *Rolling Stone*, and "pray to have even one friend. . . . But never once did it occur to me to go back home. Never."

In late November 1978, Pearl Lang invited Madonna to study and perform with her in the city. Lang was instantly impressed with Madonna's "gaminelike" qualities and cast her as a Holocaust victim in her theatrical piece *I Never Saw Another Butterfly*. "She was emaciated enough to pass for a Jewish child in the ghetto," Lang recalled. "And she danced marvelously." Lang especially remembered Madonna for a single pose she struck in another of her pieces, *La rosa en flores.* "It involves a very dramatic, high arch in the back. Madonna did it so beautifully, I can still see her dancing that role and doing that movement in my mind's eye," Lang said.

The relationship between Madonna and Lang, however, was dramatic and often volatile. The young dancer had a fierce and quick-flaring temper and constantly challenged her teacher's authority by skipping classes or showing up late. "It was like watching two tigresses prowling around, sizing each other up," one dancer remembered. The two argued frequently, and several times Madonna became so furious that she walked out in the middle of class. In one instance, after Lang made her endlessly repeat a difficult sequence, Madonna became so infuriated that she banged her head against the wall and screamed, "Is that what you want? Is that better?" Lang tolerated this behavior because, she said, "That intensity is the first thing I look for in a dancer, and Madonna had it."

In fact, after only a few months in New York, Madonna was already questioning whether she had a future in modern dance, and she began to search for other, more promising, pursuits. She had supported herself as a nude model for photography and drawing classes, as well as for private artists. She also thought more about a career in acting, a medium she had always wanted to explore. She went to "cattle calls"—open auditions attended by hundreds of hopeful actors—but was turned down for many roles, including one in the television show *Fame*. In the midst of all this, she met Dan Gilroy, who would further influence her toward a career in music.

Madonna and Dan Gilroy met in 1978 at a party. The meeting had been arranged beforehand by Norris Burroughs, an old boyfriend of Madonna's, who thought she and Gilroy would get along. Gilroy, too, was a young artistic type—a musician/songwriter/comedian whose offbeat, thrift-shop style of dress complemented Madonna's penchant for wearing men's pajama pants with high heels and costume jewelry. The two got along well and began seeing each other, spending a good deal of time at the renovated synagogue that Gilroy and his brother, Ed, shared in the New York City borough of Queens.

During the time they spent together, Gilroy taught Madonna simple chords on the guitar, and she became interested in writing her own songs. Strumming her first chord on a guitar "really clicked something off in my brain," recalled Madonna. It occurred to her that music might provide the alternative route to stardom she had been seeking, as she was growing increasingly tired of the grueling, competitive regimen required to make the grade as a professional dancer.

New York offered a wide variety of musical choices in the late 1970s. Disco was at its height, and clubs like Xenon, Studio 54, Regine's, and Danceteria were packed every night. Hordes of people danced the night away to the pulsing tunes of Donna Summer, Sylvester, and Gloria Gaynor. Yet, not too many blocks downtown from these discotheques, the punk and new wave scenes were just starting to flourish. The Ramones and Talking Heads were gaining a huge following at nightclubs like CBGB and the Mudd Club. The Sex Pistols, a British punk band known for their songs about anarchy and for the outrageous behavior of guitarist Sid Vicious, were exposing American audiences to a whole new loud and angry type of music. Madonna had been involved in the nightclub scene since her forays to gay discos with Christopher Flynn, beginning at the age of 15. She already knew she could quickly gather a crowd with her provocative dancing. Why not put her talent to good use?

In early 1979, Madonna auditioned for a video as a backup dancer for a popular European disco sensation named Patrick Hernandez. "We saw right away that she had more punch than the others," Hernandez remembered. "Instead of selecting her to dance like an idiot behind me, we separated her from the other performers."

Twenty-five hundred invitees turned out for the opening of Xenon, a New York discotheque that featured a descending "spaceship" created by Douglas Trumbull, the special effects designer for the movie *Close Encounters of the Third Kind*. Madonna's move to New York in 1978 coincided with the peak of the disco craze.

Hernandez, who had a 1979 disco hit called "Born To Be Alive," had been discovered by two Frenchmen, Jean Van Lieu and Jean Claude Pellerin. Van Lieu and Pellerin were immediately captivated by the young, vivacious Madonna and had visions of making her a disco star as well. In May 1979, less than a year after she had arrived in New York City, Madonna was whisked off to Paris, France, by Van Lieu and Pellerin.

On their arrival in Paris, Van Lieu and Pellerin made a great show of taking Madonna to parties and night-

Chrissie Hynde (right) and Pete Farndon of the Pretenders exemplified the raw, driving style of music that arose in the late 1970s in opposition to the glitzy, commercial, disco trend. Although Madonna would later become the queen of disco-influenced dance music, she originally modeled herself after punk rock musicians such as Hynde.

clubs, where they would pat her on the head and say, "Look what we found in the gutters of New York." It became increasingly apparent to Madonna that her dance career was not foremost in Van Lieu's and Pellerin's minds. She loved the nightlife as much as she had in New York, but was frustrated by the fact that she was not working at all. According to Patrick Hernandez, "It came as a big surprise to her that we wanted to turn her into a singer." Madonna and her self-appointed mentors could not even agree on dance movements. At the time, the music and style of punk rock held far more appeal to her than disco. "We wanted her to dance like Donna Summer," Hernandez recalled, "and Madonna wanted to move otherwise."

In a 1984 interview, Madonna said that she had been wildly excited about the glamorous offer that Van Lieu and Pellerin had made her. According to Madonna, "They said, 'Come to Paris, we'll give you everything you want. You'll live like a queen, we'll give you a vocal coach and you'll decide what direction you want to go in.' I did live like a queen and they did give me anything I wanted. It was the only time I lived comfortably my entire life." Yet, even with regular vocal and dance training, Madonna felt stifled. She realized that she was just another addition to the Hernandez entourage. While the whirlwind life of Paris was incredibly exciting, she was afraid her creative energies would stagnate.

Unhappy with her situation, Madonna tested her patrons' patience by demanding more and more money for the expensive clothes she desired, and they gave in to her. She also snubbed the parties and events they wanted her to attend. Van Lieu and Pellerin were not fazed by her actions, but neither were they making progress with her performing career. Meanwhile, Madonna became increasingly homesick, more so every time she received one of Dan Gilroy's witty letters. She later described him as her "saving grace," claiming his humorous letters "really made me feel good."

After a brief tour of Tunisia in North Africa, where she performed as a backup dancer for Patrick Hernandez, Madonna fell seriously ill with pneumonia. The sickness prompted her to ask her French backers for a leave of absence so she could recuperate back home. Because she was not bound by any contract to Van Lieu and Pellerin, they had no choice but to grant her request, and Madonna returned to New York.

4 ★ Into the Groove

IN AUGUST 1979, after three months away from each other, Madonna and Dan Gilroy became romantically involved again. Because Madonna had no place to live when she returned to New York, she spent most of her time at the converted synagogue, where Gilroy now taught her to play drums. Madonna described this period as her "intensive musical training. . . . It was one of the happiest times of my life. I really felt loved." Eventually, she moved in with the Gilroy brothers and began practicing drums for several hours a day. Before long, she suggested they form a band. Ed Gilroy would play guitar, with Madonna and Dan alternating on drums and vocals. After auditioning some musicians, Madonna asked her friend Angie Smit, who was a dancer, to play bass, and in the fall of 1979, the group began performing around New York. It took a while to settle on a name, but they eventually chose the Breakfast Club, inspired by their pattern of rehearsing all night and then going out to breakfast at a local coffee shop. Now that Madonna realized music was the art she wished to pursue, she put herself on a fast track.

Early in her career, Madonna dressed in clothing gleaned from thrift shops and presented herself as an irrepressible street urchin.

Madonna became the self-appointed manager of the Breakfast Club, spending hours on the phone every day arranging appearances. As always, she was her own best promoter. Dan Gilroy recalled, "She'd be up in the morning, a quick cup of coffee, then right to the phones, calling up everybody—everybody. Everyone from [record dealer] Bleecker Bob's to potential management. Anything and everything." She eventually convinced the Gilroy brothers to let her out from behind the drums to sing front and center. They were not entirely comfortable with their decision, however. This and other tensions wore on the band, and, within a few months of forming, the Breakfast Club broke up.

By late 1979, Madonna's relationship with Gilroy was dissolving—although amicably—along with the band. Oddly enough, it was just then that Madonna's former boyfriend, Steve Bray, called from Michigan to say he was moving to New York. Madonna had been considering forming a band of her own, and she needed a drummer. The timing could not have been better.

Meanwhile, Madonna had been simultaneously pursuing an acting career. In 1980, after landing some bit parts in music videos, she saw an advertisement for a role in a small independent film called *A Certain Sacrifice*. The role called for a "young, dark, fiery woman, dominant, with lots of energy, who can dance and is willing to work for no pay." Madonna wrote a detailed letter to director Stephen Lewicki, explaining why she thought she was right for the role. Once again, Madonna's bold self-promotion worked. She got the part.

In August 1980, Lewicki began shooting his film, which was an avant-garde thriller. Madonna played Bruna, a rape victim seeking revenge against her attacker. Bruna has a love interest, Dashiell, played by Jeremy Pattnosh, and together with a trio whom she calls her "family of lovers," they plot her revenge. The film con-

A youthful Madonna struts her stuff on the dance floor.

tains some scenes that are very sexually explicit, and it ends with a scene featuring a ritual sacrifice. Madonna committed a great deal of time and energy to Lewicki's film and asked only for $100 when she was called in to do some extra scenes two years after the initial filming.

45

Along with her nude modeling, Madonna's part in Lewicki's "art" film, which was revealing enough to be construed as pornographic, would unfortunately come back to haunt her once she became well known. Two of the photographers for whom she had posed, Martin Schreiber and Lee Friedlander, eventually sold their photos to *Penthouse* and *Playboy* magazines, although they had photographed her under the auspices of making art. After Madonna became famous, Lewicki attempted to release *A Certain Sacrifice,* which resulted in a legal struggle with Madonna, who preferred that her name be removed from the film.

In early 1981, after filming *A Certain Sacrifice,* Madonna formed a new band with Steve Bray. She originally wanted to call the band simply Madonna, but Bray disagreed. They were briefly called Emanon ("no name" in reverse) and then Emmy, which was one of Madonna's nicknames. Her style at this point was still closer to punk rock than to disco or dance music. According to Bray, "She was playing really raucous rock and roll, really influenced by the Pretenders and the Police. She used to really belt."

The band was soon playing gigs at clubs around the city, including My Father's Place and Max's Kansas City. Madonna and Bray rented a work space in the Music Building on New York City's Herald Square. Many musicians had studio space there, and, in order to cut corners, Madonna and Bray—who had become intimate again—began sleeping there as well. As always, money was tight. Madonna had held jobs in the city (she had worked for a while at Dunkin' Donuts and then for a short time as a coat-check girl at the ritzy Russian Tea Room), but she was so consumed by her desire to further her career as a musician that full-time work was difficult to fit in. She and Bray lived mainly on popcorn and fruit, while writing and recording music together. To this day,

Madonna always has a bowl of fresh popcorn in the living room of her California house.

One day in 1981, while riding an elevator in the Music Building, Madonna met rock promoter Adam Alter and remarked to him how much he resembled the late John Lennon. Alter and his partner, Camille Barbone, managed Gotham Productions, whose offices were also in the Music Building. Barbone, too, had previously encountered this pixielike woman in the elevator. At the time, Madonna had mysteriously asked a baffled Barbone, "Did you do it yet?" Another time, when Barbone was searching for her keys to the corridor that housed her office, Madonna opened the door for her and coyly said, "Someday you'll be opening doors for me."

Meanwhile, Alter had listened to Madonna's demo tape, which she and Steve Bray had produced. The tape included an early version of "Burning Up," a song that would become one of her first hits. Alter was very excited about Madonna's music and played the demo for Barbone. After seeing Madonna in rehearsal, Barbone promised to come watch her band perform upstairs at Max's Kansas City. The night of the gig, however, Barbone fell ill with a migraine and did not make it to the show. The next day Madonna stormed into Barbone's office, screaming, "You're just like everyone else. How could you not show up? This is my life." As startling as it was, Madonna's fiery response impressed Barbone, and she made sure she attended the next show. Madonna's presence onstage truly fascinated Barbone, who joined Madonna at the bar between sets and asked, "How would you like a manager?" Madonna squealed with delight and threw her arms around Barbone.

Madonna signed a contract with Gotham Productions on St. Patrick's Day, 1981. Since moving to New York, she had rarely had a comfortable place to live for any extended period of time. Her transient living conditions had put her into potentially dangerous situations more than once. One cold night, for example, while sleeping in an illegal space, she was forced to flee from a fire sparked by the space heaters with which she had encircled her sleeping area.

When Madonna signed her contract, Camille Barbone took the young singer under her wing. She helped Madonna find a room across the street from Madison Square Garden, in the heart of midtown Manhattan. This noisy, teeming neighborhood was a far cry from the luxury Madonna would become accustomed to later in her career. But the young singer marveled at the thought of a place of her own, even if it was just short of a flophouse.

Madonna became close with Barbone as quickly and intensely as she had with Christopher Flynn. In many ways, Barbone took care of Madonna. She acted as a friend, a sister, and a mother to her. Although Madonna often behaved in ways that infuriated Barbone—such as the time she spray-painted Barbone's pet poodles orange and pink during a tedious house-sitting weekend—Madonna's manager felt maternal toward her 22-year-old protégée. After Madonna's Thirtieth Street apartment was broken into, Barbone arranged for Madonna to live on the Upper West Side of Manhattan and began paying Madonna a $100-a-week salary. Barbone also helped Madonna obtain a housekeeping job to tide her over, took her to the dentist and the doctor, and brought her along for day trips to the beach on Long Island. For all her leniency and care, Barbone had one strict professional stipulation: Madonna was not to become romantically involved with any of her musicians after they had officially formed Madonna's backup band.

According to Barbone, Gotham Productions poured almost all of its money into promoting Madonna, getting her respectable gigs, and making a demo for her and Steve Bray. However, although Gotham had gone nearly bankrupt promoting her, Madonna split with Barbone in 1982. Madonna and Bray had discussed the Gotham arrangement and realized they did not want to make the kind of music Barbone believed would sell. Madonna felt that Barbone would not let her explore her own musical ideas. While still under contract to Gotham, Madonna had recorded a demo that included four songs—"Get Up," "Society's Boy," "Love on the Run," and "I Want You." When she broke her contract, a legal battle ensued over the copyright of these four songs. To date, the rights to the tape still have not been decided.

By 1982, Madonna had moved to the East Village, a neighborhood in the southeastern part of Manhattan. Formerly known as the Lower East Side, this area was spotted with ethnic enclaves, including Hispanic, Eastern European, and Jewish neighborhoods. In the 1970s

A somewhat stunned audience at the Ritz in New York City reacts to one of Madonna's early incarnations.

49

and 1980s, artists of all types took advantage of the East Village's relatively inexpensive rents. Madonna thrived in this atmosphere and found her niche amid the neighborhood's hip music clubs, cafés, and restaurants. She spent a lot of time with the up-and-coming graffiti artists who were a large part of the scene. Madonna carried a felt-tipped marker with her at all times, and took on the "tag" (graffiti nickname) of Boy Toy. Later, this name became synonymous with Madonna, as she wore a "Boy Toy" belt buckle for much of her early career. Although many people found this offensive, the singer insisted that it was just a joke. She explained that the label did not mean she was a toy for boys; to her, it meant "I toyed with boys." The provocative nature of the phrase's ambiguity, and the controversy it caused, only amused her.

In the early 1980s, graffiti artists were closely tied to the club scene and the world of fine art. Graffiti—inscriptions or drawings made on a public surface, such as a wall—became a sort of guerrilla form of personal expression. In the early 1980s, graffiti was becoming recognized as an art form and acknowledged for the cultural statements it made. Madonna was fascinated by the atmosphere and the people of this world.

At the same time, Madonna was determined to push her music on her own. She and Bray had cut their own demo tape, with four selections: "Ain't No Big Deal," "Stay," and early versions of "Everybody" and "Burning Up." One of her favorite night spots in 1982 was New York's Danceteria, a multilevel disco featuring live music, videos, and dancing, and frequented by such celebrities as Andy Warhol and the up-and-coming graffiti artist Keith Haring. "We'd pick out the cute boys, go right up and without saying a word kiss them on the mouth," Madonna's frequent nightclubbing companion Erica Bell told biographer Christopher Andersen. "Then we'd take their phone numbers, walk away, and while the guy was still watching, crumple up the number and throw it away."

It was at Danceteria that Madonna met Maripol, a French jewelry designer who helped introduce the singer to the so-called beautiful people—people who are identified with international society. Maripol would be responsible for much of the jewelry—huge crucifix earrings and necklaces—that became one of Madonna's trademarks.

Soon after her split with Camille Barbone, Madonna began seeing Mark Kamins, a DJ at Danceteria and an aspiring producer with connections in the recording industry. As a freelance scout for Island Records, he had discovered and signed several bands, including Ireland's U2, who would go on to become one of the label's biggest bands. Kamins listened to the four-song tape Madonna and Bray had made. All four tracks on the tape impressed him, especially "Ain't No Big Deal." Kamins offered to try to get Madonna a recording contract if she promised to let him produce her first record, and she readily agreed.

Island Records was not interested in the tape, so Kamins approached Warner Brothers, for whom he had just completed the production of David Byrne's newest album. Kamins persuaded Warner executive Michael Rosenblatt to come see the young singer, telling him Madonna would "knock you out." Rosenblatt was affiliated with Sire Records, a subsidiary of Warner Brothers. He was likely to appreciate an act like Madonna's because he had been responsible for signing George Michael's first group, Wham!, and the B-52s.

A few days later, Madonna and Kamins met with Rosenblatt in Rosenblatt's New York office, where they played the demo tape for him. After listening to the four songs, Rosenblatt felt the music was good, but not outstanding. "But here was this girl sitting in my office, radiating that certain something. Whatever it is, she had more of it than I'd ever seen. I knew that there was this star sitting there." Kamins, Rosenblatt, and Madonna then drew up a rough draft of a contract.

Rosenblatt was so eager to begin working with Madonna that he immediately took the tape to Seymour Stein, president of Sire Records, who was in the hospital recuperating from heart surgery. Stein's approval was required for all new projects. After hearing the tape, Stein was so excited that he arranged a hospital-room meeting with Madonna and Kamins the very next day.

The contract Madonna signed with Sire Records included an advance of $5,000, plus royalties and a publishing fee of $1,000 for each song she wrote. At last, Madonna had reached the end of her struggle. She would never again have to rummage for food from garbage cans, or live on a diet of popcorn. Instead of relaxing and enjoying her relative wealth, however, she immediately invested $2,500 in a Roland synthesizer.

The deal Madonna cut with Sire Records provided for a series of singles (45s), the success of which would determine whether an album would eventually be made. Sire chose to debut Madonna with "Ain't No Big Deal," with "Everybody" on the B side. When Warner Brothers heard the final cut of "Ain't No Big Deal," however, they were sorely disappointed. They decided instead to put "Everybody" on both the A and B sides. Their idea worked. "Everybody," a rousing dance tune, soon sky-rocketed up the dance charts, eventually peaking at number three.

After she signed her contract with Warner Brothers, Madonna decided she wanted to be managed by Freddy DeMann, because he handled the biggest star in pop music, Michael Jackson. Stein arranged a meeting with DeMann, who, unbeknownst to Madonna, no longer managed Jackson. Madonna burst into DeMann's office and auditioned for him on the spot. Though DeMann later said that "she has that special magic that very few stars have," Madonna did not win him over instantly. Her brash, no-nonsense attitude did not at first appeal to him. He just shook his head and said, "Who is this girl? Who in the hell does she think she is?" In the end, however, DeMann agreed to take Madonna on.

Steve Bray, who had worked with her from the beginning, assumed that he would produce Madonna's first singles, and he was surprised and angered when she gave the production job to Mark Kamins. Bray was asked to perform as a backup musician, but he flatly refused, and he and Madonna parted on bad terms. Bray would eventually return to collaborate with Madonna on future projects, however. "The relationship's too old to have something like that stand in its way," he explained. Unlike many of her one-time collaborators, Bray said he did not feel used by Madonna. "Exploited? Some people say that, but that's resentment of someone who's got the drive. It seems like you're leaving people behind or you're stepping on them, and the fact is that you're moving and they're not."

With Madonna's singles climbing up the charts, Warner Brothers approved the production of a 12-inch mini-LP. Once again, Madonna needed to decide on a producer. Although Mark Kamins had produced the wildly successful single, "Everybody," Madonna insisted on hiring a producer with more experience. She chose Reggie Lucas, who had produced records for Stephanie Mills, among others. This time it was Kamins who would feel left behind. "Yes, I was hurt, and very pissed off!" said Kamins. "She wanted someone who was better on vocals, and she was right. That's not my forte. But it was the way it was handled. Madonna never told me to my face that I was replaced by Reggie Lucas. I had to find out from the guys at Warner." Still, he did not harbor enough ill feelings to end their relationship.

"Jellybean" Benitez (left) and Madonna pose with an associate at Sigma Studios in 1982. Benitez, a rising star in the music industry, produced Madonna's hit single "Holiday." Madonna enjoyed both a romantic and professional relationship with the young DJ/producer.

When it was time to design the cover art, the executives at Warner Brothers were in a quandary. On first hearing Madonna's music, many radio and record industry people had assumed from the sound of her voice and the style of her music that she was black. The industry marketed Madonna, therefore, to a crossover audience. In fact, most of Madonna's early airplay was on black radio stations. According to Kamins, record executives were worried that she might lose her black audience if the

public knew off the bat that she was white. Consequently, they released the mini-LP with a Warholesque cover featuring a version of Madonna in every color of the rainbow.

If the 12-inch record, which included "Burning Up" and "Physical Attraction," sold well, Warner Brothers would make a full-length album. But first they wanted to make a video for "Everybody." Unfortunately, the company had budgeted a mere $1,500 for this video, not knowing that in a few years Madonna would make videos for more than 10 times that amount. Nevertheless, Madonna choreographed the video, and, in a move that was testament to the professionalism for which she would become known, coolly rechoreographed the piece when one of her three dancers did not show up for the shoot. Shortly thereafter, Warner Brothers began planning a debut album, which executives estimated might sell around 250,000 copies.

Madonna had written "Lucky Star" as a tribute to Mark Kamins for his help in furthering her career. Initially, Warner Brothers thought *Lucky Star* should also be the title of her first album. Eventually, however, they chose to capitalize on the name Madonna was making for herself by naming the album simply *Madonna.*

Meanwhile, Madonna's supercharged personal life continued at full speed. In addition to her serious, long-term relationships with both Dan Gilroy and Steve Bray, Madonna had many boyfriends, some more serious than others, but few who rated as soul mates. In the early 1980s, she had relationships with graffiti artists Jean-Michel Basquiat and Michael Stewart.

In the spring of 1983, however, around the time she was becoming known on the music scene, Madonna was seeing John "Jellybean" Benitez, who was a producer of disco hits and a DJ at a New York club called the Funhouse. When her upcoming album was short one cut

(Warner Brothers, still unsatisfied with "Ain't No Big Deal," had decided to delete it), Benitez provided her with a song called "Holiday." Curtis Hudson and Lisa Stevens of the group Pure Energy had written the song, and Benitez had already offered it to some other singers, including Mary Wilson, formerly of the Supremes. Madonna loved "Holiday," and with Benitez producing, it became the album's first single and one of her biggest hits.

Madonna and Benitez had a highly charged, very visible romance. They were known as much for their devotion to each other as for their mutual penchant for jealousy and public arguments. Theirs was, in a way, a media-ready relationship. Both were the current darlings of the New York club scene, and both were just beginning to get their feet wet in the pop music world. It was a testimony to Madonna's feelings for Benitez that he was the first New York boyfriend she ever brought home to Michigan. A *Rolling Stone* interviewer asked Benitez in 1984 why his bond with Madonna was so strong when so few of her other relationships had lasted. "We both started to move at the same pace," he replied. "My career has exploded within the industry, and hers has exploded on a consumer basis. We're both very career oriented, very goal oriented."

Critics initially dismissed the July 1983 release, *Madonna,* as a run-of-the-mill disco album. Though the singles preceding it had been incredibly popular, the LP itself was not making as much of an impact on its intended audience. Madonna took it upon herself to get the album national exposure, performing the lead single, "Holiday," in dance clubs around the country. It crept up the charts over the next eight months. Her next two singles, "Lucky Star" and "Borderline," exploded into the top 10. In fact, "Lucky Star" became the first of five straight top 10 hits for Madonna. The only other music group in recent history to have accomplished such a feat had been the Beatles. But Madonna would do them one better. Just a few short years after the days when she had been eating out of garbage cans, Madonna would become the most talked-about woman in America. Her singles would so dominate the pop charts that she eventually achieved a record that even the Beatles could not match: 15 consecutive top 5 singles.

5 Borderline

ONE OF THE BIGGEST FACTORS in Madonna's sudden emergence into stardom was her savvy use of the music video. The cable channel MTV was still relatively new in the mid-1980s, and few female stars had yet been featured on the station. Madonna changed that in a hurry.

Her first big-budget video came when Seymour Stein financed a laser- and special effects-filled video for "Burning Up." It featured shots of a chained Madonna, gyrating and singing soulfully in the middle of the road while a blond man races toward her in a convertible. Much has been made of the video's imagery by both pro- and anti-Madonna forces. Many objected to the sadomasochistic imagery and submissive lyrics, such as "Unlike the others, I'll do anything." But the most significant point of the video, in Madonna's opinion, comes at the end when, just before she is run down in the street, Madonna suddenly appears behind the wheel of the car—alone—and drives off, smirking and fully in control. Even at such an early point in her career,

Madonna opens her first national tour in Seattle, Washington, in April 1985.

the key elements of Madonna's persona are fully evident: seemingly offering herself, even degrading herself, she transforms her supposed sexual availability into a taunting celebration of her own power.

Her wish to be aggressively, seductively sexual—yet fully in control—was acted out in her personal life. One of her jilted lovers, Steve Newman, would later say, "Steve Bray told me that Madonna taught him never to trust a woman. Madonna indulges in everybody's fantasies—but only for a short while, until she becomes bored. Then she moves on to the next man, or woman—the next fantasy. She plays everybody every which way." Madonna's constant flirting and other seductive behavior has been interpreted in many ways. Some see her continual demands for attention, combined with a resolute independence and refusal to become attached to anyone, as a continuing struggle against the painful early loss of her mother or as an attempt to resist her own need for her father's attention and approval. At a purely practical level, of course, her behavior with men (and women) has not only gained her attention, but furthered her career. Almost all of the people she has seduced have had some useful connections or expertise.

Mark Kamins reported, "Madonna always had at least three guys going at a time. Each one of us was there to fulfill a separate need in her life. For a while it was me, Jellybean, and [artist-musician] Ken Compton. The cast of characters changed practically every week. There was jealousy, sure. We didn't like it, but we knew what she was doing." Ironically, Madonna chose Ken Compton to play the driver who bears down on her, but never reaches her, in the *Burning Up* video.

Her video for "Lucky Star" was a more sparse piece that featured Madonna dancing with two male dancers against a stark white background. Madonna's most elaborate video in connection with her first album was *Bor-*

derline, although it was simple compared to pieces she would be filming later in her career.

Borderline was directed by Mary Lambert, with whom Madonna worked often after their first venture together. The video tells the story of a tough, streetwise girl, played by Madonna, who is discovered by a fashion photographer. After Madonna's character enters the world of high fashion, she is stung by pangs of longing for her old life downtown. She defiantly spray-paints graffiti on the photographer's car and returns to her old life and old friends. *Borderline* was the first real "story" video that Madonna made.

Rosanna Arquette (left) starred with Madonna in the film *Desperately Seeking Susan.* After being cast in the leading role, Arquette was unhappy about having to share top billing with the rising pop star.

Meanwhile, as her *Madonna* album was selling millions of copies, Madonna had auditioned for the title role in a film called *Desperately Seeking Susan,* directed by a young filmmaker named Susan Seidelman. Seidelman was best known for *Smithereens,* a low-budget film about two sisters, one a New Jersey housewife, the other an aspiring rock and roll musician. For her new movie, Seidelman had already cast Rosanna Arquette to play the role of an amnesiac housewife who unwittingly switches identities with Susan, a woman she has secretly been following. One of the reasons Madonna was so perfect for the role of Susan is that she is very much like the character the screenwriter, Leora Barish, envisioned. Susan is a cocky, hip, mysterious woman, whom men fall in love with instantly. In fact, the film's costume designer, Hollywood veteran Santo Loquasto, outfitted the character of Susan with many items chosen directly from Madonna's own wardrobe.

When Madonna auditioned for the part of Susan in *Desperately Seeking Susan,* Seidelman had already tested many other proficient actresses for the role. "Madonna wasn't famous when we cast her," the director told *Film Comment.* "I knew her from different rock clubs, and I have musician friends who knew her. There was always something about her persona that appealed to me. She lived down the street at the time, and I kept seeing her face. Finally we got together, and I realized she was as smart as I hoped she would be. . . . She was intriguing. . . . She's a performer. She was at ease in front of the camera."

Although the *Madonna* album sold slowly at first, sales grew steadily, and eventually it became a huge hit. *Desperately Seeking Susan* was also destined to do well, but not primarily because of the box office draw of the star, Rosanna Arquette. It was due to the attraction of Madonna—the young woman clad in layered T-shirts, fingerless lace gloves, and rosaries hanging down to her always-exposed navel—that would make this movie a smash.

As Madonna was shooting her first feature film on location in New York, she began to experience the reality of her newfound fame. Except for the ill-fated *A Certain Sacrifice,* Madonna had appeared in only one other film, a movie called *Vision Quest.* But in that film, Madonna simply played herself, singing her ballad "Crazy For You" during a club scene. *Desperately Seeking Susan* was her first true acting role.

Although Madonna always appeared brash and outgoing in public, her demeanor during the making of Susan Seidelman's film could not have been more proper. She was up before dawn every day to work out before showing up for the early-morning shoot. On the set, she was professional and focused on her work. The truth was that she was extremely nervous. "A few times I was so nervous I opened my mouth and nothing came out," she told *Rolling Stone.* "I think I surprised everybody, though, by being one of the calmest people on the set at all times. I think that had to do with the fact that I was in total wonderment: I was gonna soak everything up."

Like a Virgin, Madonna's second album, came out in 1984, just before *Desperately Seeking Susan* began filming. Once again, for professional reasons, Madonna wiped her slate clean of the people who had pushed for her and worked on her first album. *Madonna* producer Reggie Lucas found himself in the same position Kamins and Bray had been in. Instead of Lucas, Madonna chose Nile Rodgers to produce *Like a Virgin.*

The *Like a Virgin* album was gaining Madonna a great deal of attention right at the height of the film's shooting schedule. When fans learned that a scene was to be filmed at a certain New York nightclub, hundreds showed up, hoping to get a glimpse of the star. And when Seidelman needed a song to use during the club scene, she chose Madonna's unreleased "Into the Groove." Though Madonna's was only a supporting role, it was soon clear that she and Arquette were being marketed as equal draws for the film.

Desperately Seeking Susan proved to be a "sleeper," a term applied to small-budget films that do extremely well at the box office. *Newsweek* magazine said the film was "as warm and ephemeral as a rainbow. . . . It's the ambience and charm of this comedy you remember as much as the gags." Pauline Kael, writing in the *New*

Yorker magazine, said "Nobody comes through in the movie except Madonna, who comes through as Madonna," adding that the actress had "dumbfounding aplomb."

Everything, it seemed, had improved for Madonna by mid-1984—her living conditions, the production budgets of her albums and videos, and her status as an actress. After her debut album brought her recognition and financial rewards, she traded the East Village address for a posh loft in SoHo, a trendy downtown neighborhood in New York City.

Madonna had been on the edge of major stardom ever since the release of her first album. By the time she had

A young, provocatively dressed Madonna frolics before a sold-out crowd in Worcester, Massachusetts, in 1985.

begun filming *Desperately Seeking Susan,* people already recognized her on the street, on the subway, and in her favorite New York hangouts. After the success of *Like a Virgin,* she was officially a superstar. She could not ride the subway anymore, but she could look out the taxi window and see many young women imitating her distinctive style of dress. It is impossible to deny the impact that Madonna's unique way of dressing had on her young female fans. Teenage girls suddenly sported layers of ripped T-shirts cut to the midriff, tousled curly hair tied up with a scarf, miniskirts, torn tights, fishnet stockings, and pumps with heels as high as their school dress codes would allow. Madonna's signature "Boy Toy" belt could be seen draped around the hips of hordes of young Madonna "wanna-bes."

In an article in the *New Republic* in 1985, Joel D. Schwartz wrote of Madonna's controversial ability to project both innocence and decadence. "Her popularity," he stated, "transcends the labels and factions that currently partition the adolescent music scene, and it is just conceivable that she is on her way to becoming a latter-day Elvis—the central icon of mid-to-late-teen popular culture." Although many feminists were outraged over the image Madonna presented, it seemed that she had become a true cult figure overnight.

Meanwhile, Madonna was preparing for her first major tour, which she entitled the Virgin tour, and continued to lead a whirlwind social life. Her stormy on-again-off-again relationship with Jellybean Benitez had lingered on throughout the filming of *Desperately Seeking Susan,* but she was also seeing several other men.

With the release of *Like a Virgin,* Madonna fans saw their idol undergo the first in a never-ending series of transformations. Her physical appearance was similar to the image she had created on her first album, but her music was different. The first album had been firmly rooted in the disco tradition, but the new songs called to mind girl groups of the 1960s. Whereas her first videos were somewhat raw pieces, the videos accompanying the second album were much more glamorous. Madonna chose Mary Lambert, who had worked with her on *Borderline,* to direct the 1984 video of "Like a Virgin," the album's title track and first single. In the video, Madonna is clad in an antique wedding dress and dances in a gondola floating through the canals of Venice.

In January 1985, Madonna began filming her next video, *Material Girl,* which also stars actor Keith Carradine. The video was an homage to Marilyn Monroe's performance of "Diamonds Are a Girl's Best Friend" in the 1953 movie *Gentlemen Prefer Blondes.* Draped in a red strapless gown—an exact replica of the one originally designed by Bill Travilla for Monroe, with matching elbow-length gloves and glittering jewelry—Madonna and her troupe of male dancers sing and dance on a soundstage centered on a huge staircase. From that staircase one day during filming, Madonna noticed a young movie actor standing in the shadows. Mary Lambert, who was directing the video, had invited Sean Penn to the set that day as a guest.

Penn was known as a member of the "Brat Pack," a title created by the press to describe a group of young actors (including Judd Nelson, Rob Lowe, Emilio Estevez, and Charlie Sheen) who often appeared in films together. Known for his devotion to Method acting, which emphasizes drawing on one's own experiences in order to put true feeling into a performance, the hot-tempered young actor, who is the son of producer Leo Penn and former actress Eileen Ryan, had gained recognition for his roles in *Taps, Fast Times at Ridgemont High, Bad Boys,* and *Racing with the Moon.* Madonna's friend Erica Bell later told writer Christopher Andersen in *Madonna: Unauthorized* that Madonna was equally excited that day about having met Penn, Elizabeth Taylor, and chicken magnate Frank Purdue. It would seem, then, that the feisty young actor did not make much of an impression on her. Yet, according to Madonna, she had a premonition that one day she was going to marry Penn.

Though Madonna was pointedly brusque with Penn at their first meeting, she did tell him to wait for her at the end of the day's filming and ran to get one of the roses she had been handing out to the video's crew. "This is for you," she said. After their brief meeting, Penn could not stop thinking about Madonna, and he decided to follow a friend's advice to pursue her. The two young stars began a romance that, for all their aspirations to privacy, played itself out from the first in the media. Penn flew all over the country to see Madonna at her concerts during her Virgin tour. It was clear to all that they were a couple, and yet rumors still circulated regarding Madonna's involvement with other men.

The Virgin tour, Madonna's first major musical tour, began on April 10, 1985, with the Beastie Boys as the opening act. Until then, the only live performances Madonna had done were lip-synched versions of her songs at dance clubs and on various television shows. People were openly skeptical regarding her ability to mount such an ambitious production as a full-length live concert. Madonna's manager, Freddy DeMann, made a point of booking her at moderately sized theaters, such as New York's Radio City Music Hall. DeMann could scarcely have known how large the demand for tickets to Madonna's concerts would be. To the pleasant surprise of DeMann and the tour promoters, all of the tickets to the Radio City shows sold out in a mere 34 minutes. Two shows had to be added at Madison Square Garden, a huge arena right across from the apartment where Madonna lived after she signed her first management contract with Camille Barbone. During her show there, Madonna told the story of how she used to sit in her room and think, "I wonder if I'll ever get in there."

The Virgin tour featured songs from Madonna's first two albums and incorporated live dancing as well. Backed up by a full band and performing Brad Jeffries' choreography with her two male dancers, Madonna sang all of her most popular material, including "Dress You Up," "Holiday," and "Crazy for You." The finale was a version

of "Material Girl," during which the star went from one band member to the next, collecting a variety of baubles and trinkets. Marlene Stewart designed the wedding outfit (a white crinoline skirt, a midriff top with a crucifix cut into it, and a white sequined jacket) that Madonna wore for the "Like a Virgin" number, as well as two other costumes, both of which capitalized on the layered, jewelry-laden look that Madonna had made fashionable.

A throng of Madonna "wanna-bes" gather at Macy's department store in New York City for a Madonna look-alike contest in June 1985. Early in her career, many of Madonna's biggest fans were teenage girls.

The volatile and passionate relationship between pop star Madonna and movie star Sean Penn made them a favorite target of the paparazzi and provided fodder for gossip columnists for several years.

Each night, the show closed with a prerecorded booming male voice admonishing her, "Madonna, get down off that stage this instant." Madonna's own prerecorded reply was, "Daddy, do I hafta?" When Madonna played in Detroit, Tony Ciccone appeared onstage to recite the closing lines of the show—and theatrically yank his daughter offstage.

When she was in New York, the Macy's department store opened a Madonna section, featuring cropped T-shirts and rubber crucifixes, bracelets, and other jewelry by Madonna's designer friend Maripol. The department was launched with a Madonna look-alike contest judged by Andy Warhol. A crowd of young women eager to imitate the star gathered to buy merchandise and compete in the contest, which was covered on the local television news.

Though her fans loved her, music critics gave Madonna mixed reviews for her touring debut. Respective headlines in *Rolling Stone* and the *New York Post* proclaimed, "Madonna Seduces Seattle," and "It's Madonna Magic!" On the other hand, the *Hollywood Reporter* called Madonna more "a cross between Charo and Wayne Newton than a latter-day Gina Lollobrigida/Marilyn Monroe–type."

During the tour, Madonna's relationship with Sean Penn continued to grow. The couple spent much of their time literally battling prying photographers and fans. In the three years they were together, Penn entangled himself in more than one melee with would-be shutterbugs— fights that landed the actor in jail and on probation for a period of time. It was no secret that the couple had many arguments, often in public; yet they loved each other deeply.

On Saturday morning, June 16, 1985, six months after they had first met, Penn and Madonna were in their room at the Maxwell House Hotel, in Nashville, Tennessee, where Penn was working on his next film, *At Close Range*. The singer recalled, "All of a sudden he got this look in his eyes. He was asking me to marry him, but he didn't say it out loud. I felt like I knew what he was thinking and I read his mind." Penn looked at Madonna, and she said, "Whatever you're thinking, I'll say yes to." Penn formally proposed to Madonna, and they made plans for one of the most opulent weddings of the decade.

6 ★ True Blue

MADONNA AND PENN WERE AWARE of the naysayers regarding their marriage from the beginning. In 1989, Madonna told *Rolling Stone*, "I felt that no one wanted us to be together. They celebrated our union, and then they wanted us to be apart. There were rumors about us getting a divorce a week after the wedding. We fought that."

Oddly, the announcement of Madonna's imminent marriage stunned even her closest friends. Erica Bell found out from Martin Burgoyne, Madonna's former New York roommate, who had heard the news on the radio. "All I could manage to get out of my mouth was 'What?'" Bell recalled. "She told no one that she was going to marry Penn. Even his family didn't know about it until they saw the news on TV."

Madonna's intense relationship with Penn was frightening to her close friends for a variety of reasons. Penn made no attempt to hide his homophobia, an attitude that ran directly counter to Madonna's strong support for the gay community. Many of her closest friends were gay, and she had always been a vocal advocate of safe sex and a major donor to various AIDS-related

---

Madonna performs before 100,000 fans in Philadelphia, Pennsylvania, as part of the globally broadcast Live Aid benefit concert on July 13, 1985.

73

organizations. Having lost several friends to the epidemic, Madonna felt deeply connected to the crisis. In a 1991 interview in the *Advocate,* Madonna said she also had "the most camaraderie" with homosexual men. "They are looked at as outsiders, so I relate to that," she said. "On the other hand, I feel that most gay men are so much more in touch with a certain sensitivity that heterosexual men aren't allowed to be in touch with, their feminine side. To me they're whole human beings, more so than most of the straight men I know." It therefore seemed strange that she would become involved with a man whose feelings were so openly antithetical to hers.

Madonna also seemed drawn to Penn's proclivity for violent behavior. She had always been a risk-taker and was drawn to stormy, fiery men, like Jellybean Benitez. Because of this, Madonna stood quietly by while Penn engaged in several of the fights that brought him almost as much fame as his acting. Perhaps she was even flattered that he was defending her during these fracases.

The first major incident that brought Penn's violent temper into the public eye occurred one weekend in Nashville, at the same hotel where Penn had proposed to Madonna. Two British journalists, Ian Markham-Smith and Laurence Cottrell of the London *Sun,* were parked in a car on the hotel grounds. Apparently, a rumor was circulating that Madonna was pregnant, and the press was hounding the couple more than usual. As Madonna left for her morning jog, the two reporters got out of the car and attempted to snap a photograph of her.

The trouble started when Penn threatened the writers with a large rock. "No pictures!" he yelled. "You take my picture and I'll break your . . . back with this rock!" A huge fight, consisting largely of Penn pummeling the two reporters, ensued. Afterward, Markham-Smith and Cottrell called the Nashville police, and Penn was arrested,

charged on two misdemeanor counts of assault and battery, and released on $1,000 bail.

During the summer of 1985, Madonna's name was rarely out of the newspapers. Soon after the incident at the Maxwell House Hotel, another controversial story involving photographs began to unfold. On July 7, 1985, Bill Stone, an artist for whom Madonna had posed during her days as a nude model, announced that he had sold his pictures to *Penthouse* magazine. Soon afterward, Martin Schreiber and Lee Friedlander, two other photographers for whom Madonna had modeled, announced a similar deal they had made with *Playboy*. The two magazines raced to get their pictures on the newsstands first. Madonna rose above what she considered a minor controversy and issued open statements saying that she was not ashamed of having posed for the photos.

Madonna and husband Sean Penn suffered an increasingly antagonistic relationship with the press. This confrontation occurred on June 27, 1988, before the Mike Tyson–Michael Spinks championship fight in Atlantic City, New Jersey, and ended with Penn reportedly striking a photographer.

On July 13, 1985, Madonna performed at Live Aid, an unprecedented, globally broadcast, rock and roll extravaganza. Live Aid was the brainchild of Scottish musician Bob Geldof, who was known for his work with the Boomtown Rats. Geldof had organized the concert to raise money for the millions of victims of the mid-1980s famine in the East African country of Ethiopia. This unique relief effort was first conceived at Christmastime in 1984, when a group of British pop and rock musicians came together under the name "Band Aid" to record "Do They Know It's Christmas?" David Bowie, George Michael, and Bono Vox of U2, among others, performed on the record, with the proceeds going toward feeding Ethiopia's hungry. Geldof was at the helm of this endeavor. A few months later, a group of American musicians, calling themselves "USA For Africa," made their own recording. Diana Ross, Michael Jackson, and others sang on "We Are the World," which had been written by Lionel Richie and Michael Jackson, and produced by Quincy Jones.

In July 1985, supporters of the cause held benefit concerts simultaneously at London's Wembley Arena and Philadelphia's J.F.K. Stadium. Television networks broadcast the 18-hour event internationally and provided viewers with phone numbers to call in order to place their own pledges toward the relief effort. Britain's most popular acts of the time—including The Style Council, Alison Moyet, Paul Young, and Elvis Costello—performed. Mick Jagger and David Bowie premiered a video they had done together of the 1960s hit "Dancin' in the Streets." Jagger and the Rolling Stones performed live in America, as did Tina Turner, Bob Dylan, and, of course, Madonna. Phil Collins performed at both concerts, flying from one venue to the other on the Concorde.

When Bette Midler introduced Madonna at Live Aid, she referred to her as "a woman who pulled herself up by her bra straps." Draped in her signature rosaries and wearing a long, brocaded coat despite the sweltering temperatures on the outdoor stage, Madonna swore to the audience that she would keep her clothes on. "You might hold it against me in ten years," she joked, referring to the controversy over her nude photos. Madonna then performed "Into the Groove," and "Holiday," and debuted "Love Makes the World Go Round."

In late July 1985, director Stephen Lewicki announced that he planned to market *A Certain Sacrifice,* the low-budget thriller that had marked Madonna's acting debut. According to Lewicki, Madonna had screened a final cut of the film eight months prior to his announcement and had complimented him on it. However, Madonna had decided she did not want her name used in conjunction with Lewicki's efforts. She found out that there was no legal way to keep Lewicki from marketing his film, nor could she keep him from using her name. On August 2, 1985, a judge ruled that Madonna's name could not be taken off the film because of a release form she had signed on September 20, 1980, five years earlier. *A Certain Sacrifice* was distributed to video stores, but, though Lewicki made a tidy profit from it, it received minimal recognition.

During the summer publicity blitz of 1985, Madonna and Sean Penn had been making plans for their wedding. The couple's fierce desire for privacy dictated the arrangements. Invitations, drawn by Penn's brother Michael, depicted Madonna and Penn in a caricature of the Grant Wood painting *American Gothic.* They were sent out to some 220 guests, with instructions that the location of the event would be announced only one day before the wedding. The festivities, billed as a joint birthday party, would be held on August 16, 1985—Madonna's 27th birthday, and one day before Penn's 25th.

Nancy Huang, producer Nile Rodger's girlfriend, treated Madonna to a bridal shower at Huang's New

York apartment. Men were invited to the shower, as long as they came dressed in women's clothes. In Los Angeles, Penn had a classic bachelor party, which many of his movie-star friends attended. For Madonna's final pre-wedding party, a group of friends took her to a male mud-wrestling establishment in Los Angeles.

According to biographer Christopher Andersen, wedding guest Andy Warhol leaked word to the media that the nuptials would take place at the estate of Dan Unger, an old friend of the Penn family's. Soon a phalanx of helicopters appeared, hovering over the estate as picture-hungry paparazzi snapped the murky shots that would be published the following day around the world. Reporters and photographers, dressed as catering employees, attempted to climb over the walls of the house. One eager photographer was discovered hiding in the bushes, outfitted in full camouflage. When asked if the Malibu house the newlyweds had purchased just before their wedding would have fences to avoid such nuisances, the feisty Penn sneered, "A fence, nothing. We're going to have gun towers."

But the extravagant fete was soon under way, with flowing Cristal champagne, sushi hors d'oeuvres, and food catered by Wolfgang Puck, owner of the world-renowned Spago, the most popular Los Angeles restaurant at the time. While stars as luminous as Tom Cruise, Rob Lowe, Emilio Estevez and his father, Martin Sheen, Cher, Diane Keaton, and David Letterman looked on, the couple exchanged their vows in an early evening, cliff-side ceremony. Madonna wore an off-white gown with a sash bedecked with rosebuds and semiprecious jewels, and in lieu of a veil she wore a jaunty bowler hat. Penn wore a double-breasted Gianni Versace tuxedo. After the ceremony, the guests moved into an outdoor tent to dine on caviar, broiled swordfish, rack of lamb, lobster ravioli, and curried oysters.

When the time came to cut the five-tiered hazelnut wedding cake, Madonna turned to Cher, whose own marriages had received more than their share of publicity, and quipped, "Hey you've done this before. Do you cut just one piece or do you have to slice up the whole thing?" After Madonna's sister Paula caught the bouquet, the couple sped off for their honeymoon.

During their honeymoon in the quaint California town of Carmel, the newlyweds managed to travel incognito for the first day or so. Soon, though, word of their stay got out, and their fans and the press descended on the couple. They fled to their new home in Los Angeles.

Soon after Madonna's wedding, former Beatle George Harrison sent her a script for a film called *Shanghai Surprise.* Harrison's production company, Handmade Films, had produced several successful films, including *Time Bandits, Life of Brian,* and *A Private Function.* Madonna showed the screenplay to Penn, and he liked the role of the male lead. It seemed logical that they do the project together. Madonna had already recorded a ballad entitled "Live To Tell," for Penn's upcoming film with Christopher Walken, *At Close Range,* but this was the first acting project the couple had considered doing together.

Initially, Madonna and Penn were drawn to the script because it reminded them of the "screwball comedies" of the 1930s and 1940s. Madonna has often spoken of her admiration for actresses such as Carole Lombard and Judy Holliday, whose beauty and comic abilities made them irresistible. *Shanghai Surprise* was about a young female missionary in China during the 1930s and her romance with another American, played by Penn. The chance to shoot on location in China also appealed to Madonna and Penn.

Upon arriving in Shanghai, China, on January 8, 1986, Madonna felt optimistic about working in what

Shortly after their marriage, Madonna and Penn costarred in *Shanghai Surprise*, a romantic adventure-comedy set in China during the 1930s. They were so disappointed with the final version of the film that they publicly denounced it.

she thought would be an enriching, peaceful atmosphere. "We arrived in the middle of the night," she recalled. "We couldn't sleep so we ended up just walking around in the streets on this steel-cold morning. It was still dark out, and the streets were filled with people doing tai chi. So dreamlike."

Madonna and Penn spent their first week of production in Hong Kong, where they went unrecognized by the locals. Madonna was pleased that it was her blonde hair (a rare sight in Hong Kong) rather than her well-known face that turned people's heads.

Shooting the film presented difficult challenges, however. The slums in which the crew was filming were controlled by gangsters who demanded huge sums of money at every turn. Also, Madonna said, "There were big, black rats underneath our trailers." By the end of their stay in China, Madonna and her husband were exhausted both from tensions on the set and from trying to stay out of the spotlight.

While relations with the press in Hong Kong had been peaceful, trouble started when filming began in the Portuguese port of Macao, 40 miles west of Hong Kong. There, reporters and photographers regularly hounded Madonna and Penn. They even went so far as to sneak into their hotel to surprise the couple in the hallway outside their room. More than once, Penn lost his temper and flew into a rage at the writers and paparazzi.

When the cast moved on to England, where *Shanghai Surprise* was scheduled to finish shooting, trouble continued to brew. In the onslaught of press people that greeted the February 21, 1986, arrival of Madonna and Penn, one reporter claimed that their Mercedes had run over his toe. The British press lambasted the couple every chance it got. Penn's unwillingness to pose for photos or give interviews did not help matters. Finally, George Harrison arranged a press conference in order to dispel ill will and to allow the press at least a small shot at its favorite targets. Penn did not appear at the news conference, but Madonna was there at Harrison's side. Harrison spoke well of his two stars and tried to fend off the personal questions the press was determined to ask. When one reporter asked Madonna if she and Penn fought, Harrison immediately quipped, "Do you row with your wife?" The trials of location-shooting in China were past, and the British press had been sufficiently appeased.

In a 1986 interview in *Rolling Stone,* Madonna recalled this period in her life with unhappiness, yet pointed out that what got her through it was her relationship with her husband. "Strangely enough," she reported, "we never got along better. We took turns being strong and not letting it really affect us."

Nevertheless, the final cut of *Shanghai Surprise*, released in October 1986, was a disaster in the eyes of Penn and Madonna, and they promptly disowned the film. It bombed both with the critics and in the theaters. The headline of *Rolling Stone*'s review pronounced it "Madonna's First Flop." Janet Maslin of the *New York Times* wrote, "Just because something takes up two hours worth of screen time and offers well-known people the chance to dress cleverly and talk about stolen opium and jewels and secrets of the Orient, it isn't necessarily a movie. We'd all be better off if that were more widely known."

As always, though, Madonna was already working on other projects. In the summer of 1986, just before *Shanghai Surprise* came out, Madonna released her third album, *True Blue*. Musically, the album was a departure from her first two ventures. It was the first album on which she received production credit, though it was a joint effort with Patrick Leonard and Steve Bray, with whom Madonna had reconciled. Though as danceable as ever, her songs were no longer concerned solely with a beat. Many of them now dealt with serious issues. For example, "Papa Don't Preach" is about a teenage girl who gets pregnant and defiantly chooses to have her baby. The song stirred controversy, spurring responses from groups both in favor of and against abortion rights. Oddly enough, many pro-life groups applauded Madonna for this song while Planned Parenthood opined, "The message is that getting pregnant is cool and having the baby is the right thing and a good thing and don't listen to your parents, the school, anybody who tells you otherwise. . . ."

In *Rolling Stone*'s Summer 1986 issue, reviewer Davitt Sigerson wrote a glowing review of Madonna's latest effort. He stated, "Madonna's sturdy, dependable, lovable new album remains faithful to her past while shamelessly rising above it. . . . It sets her up as an artist for the long run."

Accompanying Madonna's new sound was another new look. Her blonde hair was now cropped short. Gone was the layered, chaotic teenage look of her former persona. In its place was a sleek, pared-down version of her former self. Madonna's body, always voluptuous, had

Madonna charms "Tonight Show" host Johnny Carson after her national talk show debut in 1987. During the broadcast Madonna declared that she was "just a midwestern girl in a bustier."

been worked over with weights and training to make it as taut as possible. It seemed that she was growing up before the public's eyes.

Madonna spotlighted her new image in the video for "Open Your Heart," directed by Jean-Baptiste Mondino. In the video, Madonna plays an exotic dancer working at a peep show patronized by an odd array of men. Madonna begins the video wearing a sleek black wig, which she later removes to reveal her short, platinum blonde hair. Her costume is a black, corsetlike bodysuit, which became the staple of her wardrobe for the tour that promoted the album, and which accentuated Madonna's "new" body. The video for "Open Your Heart" features a young boy who is trying to sneak into the peep show. At the end, Madonna's character scrubs off her makeup, tousles her hair, and dances off with the young boy, both of them clad in matching men's suits and porkpie hats. The slick, polished look of Mondino's video was indicative of Madonna's new image.

In July 1987, Madonna launched her Who's That Girl? tour. The concert tour was intended to serve as a promotion for her most recent album, as well as for an upcoming movie by the same name. After her first tour, Madonna had sworn she would never go on the road again. Having changed her mind, she insisted that this trip at least be interesting for her. The Who's That Girl? tour was choreographed by Shabba Doo, a well-known break-dancer and choreographer. The costumes were by Marlene Stewart, who had designed the clothes for Madonna's first tour. Conspicuously absent were Maripol's layered chains of crucifixes and rubber bracelets.

The show included straight renditions of Madonna's hits, as well as campy, satirical versions of songs like "Dress You Up" and "Material Girl." It was a theatrical as well as a musical stage show. In addition to elaborate costume changes (one of which took place onstage in a

British-style phone booth), Madonna had a new sidekick on this concert tour. Chris Finch, a 13-year-old dancer from California, appeared with Madonna to recreate the role of the young boy from Madonna's popular *Open Your Heart* video. He danced with her during other numbers as well. Though he always behaved professionally, it was impossible to deny that he was still a teenager. When the tour stopped in his hometown of Anaheim, the requisite kiss Madonna gave him during "Open Your Heart" lasted an extremely long time, Finch recalled. "She knew all my friends were going to be there so she kissed longer than usual. I lost my place and couldn't remember the next steps in the number."

The type of controversy that was to become a trademark of her next tour also flared up on this one. In

In July 1987, Madonna brought her Who's That Girl? tour to Madison Square Garden for a benefit concert for AIDS research. She performed several seductive dance numbers on the tour with 13-year-old Chris Finch (right).

France, the tour was slated to play in Sceaux, a Paris suburb. The outdoor show was to take place on the former grounds of a royal palace, but the citizens of Sceaux were fearful of the damage unruly fans might cause to the grounds, and they rallied successfully to cancel the show. The show was reinstated, however, after the daughter of the French premier and mayor of Paris, Jacques Chirac, publicly beseeched her father to allow it to go on. Appearing at a press conference with Chirac, Madonna presented him with a major donation for AIDS research in France.

Madonna received warm reviews for her performances during the Who's That Girl? tour. It was an ambitious project, highly dependent on her numerous elaborate costume changes. On August 27, 1987, in *Rolling Stone* magazine, Vince Aletti reviewed her sold-out performance at New York's Madison Square Garden. The show was a benefit for the American Foundation for AIDS Research (AMFAR) and raised $400,000 for the organization. Aletti wrote that "Madonna, whose image was always more powerful than her voice, now sounds strong enough to belt out her most demanding material and keep going. Without losing the graininess that gives her vocal character, she's developed a rich fullness that delivers an emotional punch previously missing in her shows."

From 1986 to 1988, Sean Penn had continued his acting career, appearing in Francis Ford Coppola's Vietnam film, *Casualties of War,* with Michael J. Fox, and then as a Los Angeles police officer in Dennis Hopper's *Colors.* Many of the songs on *True Blue* had been written at the height of Madonna's romance with Sean Penn, and the album was dedicated to him. But things between Madonna and Penn, who had been married for just over two years by late 1987, were increasingly unstable. Their relationship had always been stormy, but in 1987 and 1988 their problems became more public than ever.

Around Thanksgiving Day, 1987, tensions between the couple reached an all-time high. When she was on the East Coast, Madonna spent a good deal of time with John F. Kennedy, Jr., and Penn—himself known for his flings with women—was convinced the two were romantically involved. At the same time, Penn's public outbursts had become somewhat of a personal trademark, and each time he so much as sneered at fans, photographers, or his wife, his tantrums made the newspapers.

One of the main conflicts arising in the Penn/Madonna marriage was Penn's increasing jealousy of his wife's relationship with performer Sandra Bernhard. Bernhard had started out doing stand-up comedy in the clubs of Los Angeles and had eventually moved into acting. She became widely known as an actress after her portrayal of Masha, the eccentric kidnapper in Martin Scorsese's *The King of Comedy*. In 1988, Bernhard performed in a one-woman show she had written, *Without You I'm Nothing*, which incorporated comedy, monologues, and songs. By this time, Bernhard had become something of an artistic icon, especially in the gay community, because she was open about her sexual attraction to women and her work involved breaking traditional gender boundaries. In the early 1990s, Bernhard appeared as a regular on the TV situation comedy "Roseanne," in which she played a lesbian, the first time such a character had been written for a major sitcom.

Without You I'm Nothing included a monologue about a dream in which Madonna appeared. The circumstances of the dream were peculiarly similar to a dream that Madonna had. The two quickly became friends and were often seen out together. Both Madonna and Bernhard were known for their eyebrow-raising antics. The wildest stunt they pulled was the time they appeared together, dressed alike, on "Late Night with David Letterman" in July 1988. During their banter with Letterman, they slyly implied that they might be romantically involved, but never said anything outright. It was a bold move, to be sure; the public and the media, who were not accustomed to being asked to accept the possibility that two well-known pop figures might be anything other than heterosexual, talked about the appearance for weeks afterward.

Performance artist Sandra Bernhard and Madonna perform at the Brooklyn Academy of Music to raise money to preserve the world's rain forests. The two shared a close friendship that they hinted was also a sexual relationship.

Madonna's marriage was in such turmoil by Thanksgiving Day, 1987, that Madonna, who spent the holidays at her sister's house in Brooklyn, New York, refused to see Penn. She then filed for divorce. In the early weeks of the Christmas season, the divorce papers were rescinded "without prejudice," which meant the terms could be reinstated at any time. Most of the following year was a rerun of stormy times and tearful reunions, during which Madonna and her husband tried to make their marriage work.

In the fall of 1987, *Who's That Girl?* debuted in movie theaters. Jamie Foley directed the film; he had directed Sean Penn in *At Close Range* and Madonna in the *Papa Don't Preach* video. Madonna was a great admirer of Foley's work and had been very eager to do a film with him. Once again, Madonna was trying to return to the days of the screwball comedies of the 1930s and 1940s. In 1987, she told *American Film* magazine that the reason she chose to do *Who's That Girl?* was that it reminded her of the famous Cary Grant–Katharine Hepburn film, *Bringing Up Baby* (on which *What's Up, Doc?* was later based). "I just love those films where the woman gets away with murder, but her weapon is laughter. And you end up falling in love with her," Madonna explained.

In *Who's That Girl?* Madonna played Nikki Finn, a young woman convicted of a crime she did not commit. Griffin Dunne played the buttoned-down lawyer sent to pick her up upon her release from prison. The film follows the pair over the course of a weekend of mishaps and missteps, during which, not surprisingly, they fall in love.

Unfortunately, the critics panned the picture, and no amount of media hype could turn it from a flop into a hit. In his review, Vincent Canby of the *New York Times* wrote of the tens of thousands of fans gathered in Times

Joe Mantegna (left), Madonna, and Ron Silver take their bows after a performance of *Speed-the-Plow* in 1988. The David Mamet play provided Madonna with her first Broadway role.

Square for a glimpse of Madonna on the night of the film's New York premiere. The next day, he said, barely 60 seats were filled in New York's 1,151-seat Ziegfeld Theatre. Although the movie did poorly, its soundtrack, featuring four new songs by Madonna, sold very well. The title track made it all the way to number one on the charts, and "Causing a Commotion," another song from the movie, reached number two.

So far, the only acting role that had gained Madonna any positive recognition was the one in her first major film, *Desperately Seeking Susan*. The most important people in Hollywood were not wholly against her, though. Barry Diller, then head of Twentieth Century-Fox, was quoted as saying, "Madonna is a movie star without a movie. She's such a movie star, in fact, that I'd say she's got a good ten years to find the right movie to prove it."

By the end of 1987, her list of acting credits had expanded. That year, she joined an ensemble cast that included Matt Dillon and Jennifer Grey to film Howard Brookner's production of *Bloodhounds of Broadway,* an adaptation of Damon Runyon stories that was being produced for Public Television's "American Playhouse" series. Madonna, however, had her sights set on Broadway. Though her acting work had largely been in films, Madonna was not entirely new to live theater. In 1986, she and Sean Penn had performed in an exclusive production of David Rabe's *Goose-Goose and Tom-Tom,* about three gangsters. It was a one-night-only, no-critics-allowed, invitation-only production at New York City's Lincoln Center.

In late 1987, Madonna pursued a role in David Mamet's newest play, *Speed-the-Plow,* about two ruthless Hollywood producers and the temporary secretary who enters their world. Karen, the secretary, seems at first innocent and wide-eyed, and she quickly makes a strong impression on one of the producers. In her quest to have him option a book that would make a virtually unmarketable movie, she pits the two producers against each other, thereby giving them a taste of their own seedy medicine. In the end, Karen loses out, and the producers resume their standard wheeling and dealing.

In January 1988, after a rigorous round of auditions with the playwright and the director, Gregory Mosher,

Madonna landed the role of Karen. Two established actors starred with her: Joe Mantegna, a frequent collaborator of Mamet's, and Ron Silver, who would win the 1988 Tony award for Best Actor for his role in *Speed-the-Plow.*

The play was originally scheduled to open at Lincoln Center's Mitzi E. Newhouse theater, before moving on to Broadway. When Madonna's name was added to the cast, however, ticket sales skyrocketed, and the April 6, 1988, preview date was rescheduled for Broadway's Royale Theatre.

As this was Madonna's first venture into live theater, she was prepared for a tough time with the critics. Reviews, it turned out, were mixed. Edith Oliver, writing in the *New Yorker,* said, "As for Madonna, who, for all her other credits, is just a beginner in the theater, her performance seemed to me just right." Clive Barnes, on the other hand, said that Madonna "sound[ed] more as if she were auditioning than acting, and the audition is scarcely for the big-time. There is a genuine, reticent charm here, but it is not ready to light the lamps on Broadway." Frank Rich, notorious for his scathing theater reviews, said Madonna delivered "intelligent, scrupulously disciplined comic acting." Another critic was so aghast that he demanded that Rich apologize to every actor he had ever given a bad review.

Madonna has spoken more than once regarding the challenge and difficulty of her role in *Speed-the-Plow.* In a 1989 interview with *Rolling Stone,* Madonna said of the part, "I hated to love it, and I loved to hate it. It was just grueling, having to do the same thing every night, playing a character who is so unlike me. . . . To continue to fail each night and to walk off that stage crying, with my heart wrenched. . . . It just got to me after a while. I was becoming as miserable as the character I played." As fulfilling as playing the part on Broadway had been for

Madonna, she found that toward the end of her run she "was marking days off the calendar!"

The year 1988 had been an important one, artistically, for Madonna. She had spent the year focused on furthering her career as an actress. Though she had not released a new album, she had been busy writing the songs that would comprise her next, and possibly most important, recording. However, Madonna's personal life, especially her relationship with her husband, continued to overshadow her professional efforts.

On December 28, 1988, Madonna and Penn had a confrontation that ended their marriage forever. It is not publically known what actually happened that night—various accounts with different details still circulate. Some reports claim that Penn tied up Madonna and kept her prisoner for several hours. Madonna has since refused to discuss in interviews what the tabloids refer to as her "night of terror" with Penn. Of the published accounts, Madonna says only that they are "extremely inaccurate. . . . They made it all up."

Still, it is clear that there was a major confrontation between the two that night in Madonna's Malibu house. It was so serious that Madonna went to the sheriff's office to file assault charges against Penn (which she later dropped). On January 5, 1989, Madonna refiled for divorce, sticking by her decision this time, and her union with Penn officially ended.

7 You're a Superstar

THE LINGERING, PAINFUL FEELINGS resulting from Madonna's failed marriage would not be easily forgotten. But the star did not allow her personal problems to keep her from forging ahead in her work. Many of the serious issues she had grappled with in her relationship with Penn would turn up in her next album, *Like a Prayer*. But before the album was released, Madonna took on what was for her a radically new project by agreeing for the first time to appear in a television commercial. Not coincidentally, the commercial gave Madonna the opportunity to earn a large sum of money while simultaneously introducing her new album to the public.

For years, Madonna had steadfastly refused to endorse any products, although she was more than willing to lend her time and support to worthwhile causes, such as benefits for AIDS organizations and saving the rain forest. In 1989, however, the singer finally changed her tune. On January 15 of that year, the Pepsi-Cola Corporation announced that Madonna had entered into a yearlong endorsement deal with the company. Pepsi would pay Madonna $5 million for three television spots advertising the soft drink and

---

Madonna belts out a song at London's Wembley Arena. The show required eight costume changes, but this much-discussed outfit received the most attention.

would sponsor her upcoming concert tour. In an equally momentous move, for the first time in media history a major single would be premiered in a television commercial.

The commercial, which would be one of the longest TV ads ever produced, was scheduled to make its debut on March 2, 1989. The video for "Like a Prayer," the title track from the new album, would air the following day. Pepsi was stirring up Madonna hype in full force. On February 22, during the 1989 Grammy awards, Pepsi even broadcast a commercial for the upcoming commercial. The hoopla surrounding the commercial created as much anticipation as Pepsi's campaign using Michael Jackson and the Jacksons had done a few years earlier.

Madonna said at the time, "I do consider it a challenge to make a commercial that has some sort of artistic value. I like the challenge of merging art and commerce. . . . The Pepsi spot is a great and different way to expose the record."

The television ad shows Madonna watching movies of herself as a little girl, and then the star and the girl on the screen magically change places. One segment depicts her dancing through the halls of a parochial school as an adult while singing with a gospel chorus. At the end, the adult Madonna and the child Madonna toast each other through the TV screen with a Pepsi. The commercial ended with the elder Madonna whispering, "Make a wish," Pepsi's slogan at the time. Madonna asked only that she not be shown actually drinking a Pepsi and that there be minimal shots of her holding the can.

Madonna's own video of the song, directed by Mary Lambert, bore little resemblance to the commercial. Though both featured a full gospel chorus, their story lines and images were completely different. In fact, during production of the video, Pepsi had no idea what was going to be shown on-screen. In an interview in *Forbes* magazine, Roger Mosconi, senior creative director at BBDO Worldwide Advertising, the agency that produced the commercial for Pepsi, recalled, "One day Madonna, who liked to joke with me, came up to me and said, 'Hey Roger, are you going to have the burning cross reflecting in the Pepsi can?' And I said, 'What burning cross?' And she smiled and said, 'You'll see.'"

The day after the commercial's premiere, Mosconi found out what Madonna meant. The video that debuted on MTV on March 3, 1989, was certainly a departure from the television ad. Madonna and Lambert had created a theatrical piece of cinema, in which a young African-American man is wrongly accused of attacking a white woman. The character Madonna plays witnesses the actual assault and takes refuge in a church, where she falls asleep in a pew. In her subsequent dream, a religious statue resembling the black man comes to life and passionately kisses Madonna. Upon waking, she reveals what she knows about the crime to the police. The white man who actually committed the crime is apprehended, and the cast comes out on a small stage to take a bow at the end of their mini-play.

Though the story line might have inspired debate, it was hardly controversial enough to prompt Pepsi to pull the commercial. However, interspersed with the dramatic action of the video were shots of Madonna singing against a backdrop of burning crosses—hardly an easy image for a major American corporation to swallow. The archconservative American Family Association (AFA), headed by the Reverend Donald Wildmon, found the video so offensive that the day after its premiere the AFA called for a yearlong nationwide boycott of all Pepsi products.

It is not known what brought Pepsi officials to their final decision regarding Madonna's endorsement of their product. No doubt the AFA boycott threat was an influential factor. Whatever the reason, the commercial ran only twice—both times during "The Cosby Show," a popular TV situation comedy. After this limited airing, Pepsi pulled the commercial and canceled the two subsequent Madonna spots yet to be filmed and shelved plans for backing her concert tour. This was a major move, considering that in addition to the $5 million promised to Madonna for her work, Pepsi had spent another $5 million on the production of the commercial.

When the *Like a Prayer* album was released on March 21, 1989, it was already prominent in the minds of the media and the public. On the whole, *Like a Prayer* was the most complex and polished recording Madonna had made so far. Madonna's early singles were straight dance tunes, designed to make the body move but having little effect on the intellect. On *True Blue,* Madonna had explored some serious issues with "Papa Don't Preach." But *Like a Prayer* addressed her religious faith, her mother's death, her failed marriage, and other intensely personal issues. The title track starts out with Madonna earnestly calling out, "God? God?" before the music starts. On "Till Death Do Us Part," apparently an artistic catharsis of sorts, she sings of a tumultuous marriage, and on "Promise To Try" she explores the hurt and bewilderment she felt at losing her mother as a child. In an unprecedented move for Madonna, the singer collaborated with Prince on a stylized duet called "Love Song." Each copy of the album was scented with patchouli oil to increase its religious aura.

Madonna's career had blossomed just after the advent of MTV, and she was one of the first musical artists to take full advantage of the medium. It seemed as if a Madonna song was not complete until its video had been released. Despite—or, perhaps, because of—the furor raised over her *Like a Prayer* video, her videos from then on would employ ever more controversial imagery. Her

music videos had often been openly sexual in nature, but in the late 1980s she began pushing the sexual content of her videos to new extremes.

Madonna nuzzles her boy-friend and costar Tony Ward in the controversial video *Justify My Love*, which was banned from MTV because of its explicit sexual content.

Madonna saw "Express Yourself," another track from *Like a Prayer*, as a song about women's empowerment and autonomy. In the song's video, she chose to illustrate these issues by using images of oppressed workers chained to the machine of industry, in a takeoff on the Fritz Lang film *Metropolis*. Many people saw the video's mechanical, masculine images as further illustrations of women's weaknesses, rather than as a representation of breaking those bonds. The issue of power was further muddled by Madonna's decision to wear a collar and chain in one scene.

The controversy over Madonna's hypersexual videos reached a fever pitch in 1990, when she released *Justify My Love*, a video that accompanied a song from her album *The Immaculate Collection*, released the same year. *The Immaculate Collection* was a compilation album containing two new songs and several previous hits with accompanying videotape.

"Justify My Love," cowritten with Lenny Kravitz, was a quiet, pulsing dance tune. Yet when the video, a film realization of several of Madonna's sexual fantasies, was released, it was deemed close to pornographic. Even MTV, which had always supported Madonna, refused to air it. The dreamlike video is set in a deserted hotel. As Madonna's character peers into the different rooms, she witnesses men and women engaged in sexual acts of varying types.

So great was the furor over the video that Madonna appeared on the national news show "Nightline" to make a public statement regarding her work. In the December 3, 1990, interview, "Nightline" anchorman Forrest Sawyer made reference to the *Express Yourself* video, in which Madonna crawled under a table, a huge chain and metal collar around her neck. Madonna responded by saying, "I have chained myself, though, okay? No—there wasn't a man that put that chain on me. I did it myself. I was chained to my desires. . . . I do everything by my own volition. I'm in charge."

A coterie of dancers demonstrate "vogueing," the dance phenomenon that Madonna helped popularize with the video for her hit song "Vogue." The song became the number one single of 1990.

Though *Justify My Love* had been banned by MTV, Madonna still emerged victorious. She and her manager, Freddy DeMann, chose to release the clip as the first-ever video single, which was sold in video stores for $9.95. The venture turned out to be a lucrative one—the video sold so quickly that within days of its release, stores were already ordering more.

Madonna's 1990 video, *Vogue,* was an equally stylish but less threatening homage to a dance style popular at the time in parts of the gay community. "Vogueing" had emerged from a primarily black and Hispanic subculture in New York City, just as break dancing had in the mid-1980s. Unlike break dancing, however, which had developed on street corners, vogueing was pursued by dancers affiliated with various groups called "houses," such as the House of Xtravaganza (two of whose dancers would appear on Madonna's Blonde Ambition tour), which competed at "balls," or vogueing contests. Two dancers would face off and dance competitively, freezing regularly to "strike a pose."

In comparison with many of Madonna's previous videos, *Vogue,* filmed in black and white, was a more traditional piece, featuring dance sequences choreographed by Karole Armitage and close-ups of Madonna's face, made up to resemble film stars of the 1930s and 1940s. However, the initial shot of the video showed Madonna's well-muscled back, filmed at an angle that directly mirrored "Mainbocher Corset," a picture taken by Horst P. Horst in 1939. The video also copied nine other images by the famous photographer. Horst was initially upset, but the conflict was soon smoothed over. The song sold more than two million copies and became the best-selling single of 1990. It was Madonna's eighth number one song.

Although she was becoming acknowledged as MTV's preeminent video artist, Madonna was not satisfied with the opportunities offered by the medium. Despite her mixed record as a movie actress, she still hoped to translate her success as a video artist to the big screen. Madonna had a very clear idea of what she wanted to do in Hollywood. By 1989, she owned her own production company, Siren Films, which had been created to scout prospective films in which she could act. By the late 1980s, she had already spent a few years vying for the title role in the film version of *Evita,* Andrew Lloyd Weber's musical about the poor girl who became the glamorous first lady of Argentina in the 1950s. Madonna knew that both she and Meryl Streep, among other actresses, were being considered for the title role. But negotiations were slow, and each time Madonna thought a deal had been closed, another obstacle would arise. Eventually, due to artistic differences between Madonna, producer Robert Stigwood, and Oliver Stone, who was directing the film, the deal fell through altogether.

Madonna's company was also involved in trying to develop films based on the lives of both Martha

Graham, one of the founding figures of modern dance, and Frida Kahlo, the Mexican painter whose work had burst into international prominence in the late 1980s. In 1993, Madonna still cited these projects as possibilities, though none had proceeded further than the conceptual stage.

In 1989, when Madonna heard about the role of Breathless Mahoney, the femme fatale in Warren Beatty's upcoming film *Dick Tracy,* she knew she wanted it. Madonna later said, "I saw the A-list and I was on the Z-list!" but she was intent on getting the part. She was so determined that she finally agreed to work "for scale"—the minimum pay a member of the Screen Actors Guild must receive for work. By accepting a mere $1,440 per week, Madonna was partially responsible for the extravagant film coming in under budget. This was a major concern of Beatty's, as he was still trying to regain credibility with the studios after his disastrous movie *Ishtar.* (In exchange for her low paycheck up front, Madonna negotiated a percentage of the gross income from the movie and ended up making several million dollars on the deal.) For her work in *Speed-the-Plow* and the *Like A Prayer* video, Madonna had dyed her hair back to its natural brown, and she had been enjoying her time as a brunette. However, she agreed to bleach her hair blonde again for this role.

The work she did on *Dick Tracy* expanded both Madonna's creative and personal life in many ways. The role spoke to her sense of nostalgia as an actress. She liked the idea of playing a 1930s-style femme fatale. It also altered her usual working style. Madonna was known for liking her first take best when she worked on a film, while Warren Beatty's directorial style sometimes called for a scene to be shot as many as 30 times before he was satisfied. But, as usual, Madonna won praise for her professionalism and discipline on the set.

Madonna and Warren Beatty arrive at the Washington, D.C., premiere of their film, *Dick Tracy.* Their high-profile romance brought much free publicity to the film.

The project was also virgin territory musically for the singer. Songwriter Stephen Sondheim made a rare departure from Broadway musicals to write the songs Madonna would have to sing for the movie. Sondheim is known for his quirky musical style, and his pieces present a challenge for even the most accomplished singer. Learning the songs for the film was a major test for Madonna. Acknowledging the "chromatic wildness" of the melodies, Madonna commented, "They're brilliant, but really complex." In 1990, in conjunction with the film, Madonna released a new album, *I'm Breathless: Songs from and Inspired by the Film Dick Tracy,* which also contained her hit single "Vogue."

Offscreen, Madonna was once again involved in a very visible romantic relationship. Her director and costar,

104

Warren Beatty, was well known for the romances he had shared with his leading women. Julie Christie, Diane Keaton, and Natalie Wood had all starred with Beatty at one time or another, and each had had a long relationship with him. Beatty and Madonna had begun getting to know each other during negotiations for the film, just as her marriage to Sean Penn was ending.

Soon after filming on *Dick Tracy* began, Madonna and Beatty became a couple. They even had pet names for each other (she called him Old Man; he called her Buzzbomb). Like Sean Penn, Beatty was known to be quite reserved about his private life, although not to the point of punching photographers.

It was inevitable that many media people and movie-goers would consider the relationship between director and actress to be nothing more than a publicity stunt, especially because it ended as suddenly as it had begun after the filming was completed. At that time, Madonna told Kevin Sessums of *Vanity Fair,* "Sometimes I'm cynical and pragmatic and think it will last as long as it lasts. Then I have moments when I'm really romantic and I think, 'We're just perfect together.'" Normally tight-lipped, Warren Beatty did deign to say of Madonna, "She's no accident."

Though the film received mixed reviews, *Dick Tracy* hit box office gold. Al Pacino and Dustin Hoffman, both in heavy comic-book-style gangster makeup, played supporting roles, while other stars, such as James Caan and Charles Durning, appeared in cameos. The film's creators wanted it to look like the famous comic strip come-to-life, and *Dick Tracy* was applauded for the brilliantly colored scenic design, lavish costumes, and makeup artistry used to achieve its comic-book appearance. *New York* magazine described Madonna's Breathless Mahoney as "icy, narcissistic, and grabbing." The *New Yorker* said, "She vamps entertainingly."

Madonna's greatest triumph in connection with the film came at the 1990 Academy Awards ceremony, where "Sooner or Later," a Sondheim song from the film, won the Oscar for Best Song. In true Hollywood fashion, Madonna—whose date for the awards ceremony was Michael Jackson—sang at the event, dressed in the diamond-dripping, fur-stoled style of Marilyn Monroe, one of her film idols, and her dazzling performance was the talk of the evening.

Meanwhile, Madonna had begun to prepare for her Blonde Ambition tour, which would promote her new album. Because Pepsi had withdrawn its sponsorship of Madonna's tour in 1989, this one was her first since 1987's Who's That Girl? tour. The Blonde Ambition tour, featuring new material from *Like A Prayer, I'm Breathless,* and *The Immaculate Collection,* would top her previous tours in its technical and theatrical splendor. Madonna's brother Christopher, who was gaining a reputation as a serious artist in his own right, would oversee the project's art direction. Though Karole Armitage, the cutting-edge choreographer who created the dance sequences for Madonna's *Vogue* video, was originally slated to choreograph the show, artistic differences caused Madonna to hire Vince Paterson instead.

Madonna's latest tour would also become the subject of a tell-all documentary, *Truth or Dare.* This was definitely a departure for Madonna, who was meticulous about the image she presented to her audience. But surprises are, after all, very much a part of the Madonna mystique, and once again she chose to break the rules by making the most revealing documentary of a concert tour ever made. Initially, the person most surprised by Madonna's unconventional approach was the film's director, Alek Keshishian.

When Keshishian was a senior at Harvard, his final project was an opera of Emily Brontë's *Wuthering*

Heights, using the voices of various pop and rock artists, including Madonna, Kate Bush, and Billy Idol. Hollywood agent Jane Berliner had shown Madonna a copy of Keshishian's video. Though he was only 25 years old at the time, Keshishian had already directed videos for some major stars. His credits included Elton John's *Sacrifice* and Bobby Brown's *My Prerogative.* Just weeks before Madonna's Blonde Ambition tour was to start, while Keshishian was working out a directing deal for Mariah Carey's latest video, the phone rang at his apartment. "Hi, Alek, it's Madonna," said the voice on the other end. "I don't know if you've heard, but I'm about to go on a world tour, and I was wondering if you'd like to film it." David Fincher, who had directed Madonna's videos for "Express Yourself," "Oh, Father," and "Vogue," had been slated to film some promotional footage of the tour but had backed out at the last minute, and Madonna chose Keshishian as his replacement. As far as the young filmmaker knew, this would be straight concert footage for possible use in a television special. Within three days, he was on a plane bound for Tokyo.

Keshishian began filming immediately in Japan. In addition to shooting rehearsals and performances of the show, he also filmed Madonna and her dancers backstage. Soon both he and Madonna realized that, although the performance pieces made fine cinematic material, the real essence of the project was what was going on offstage. Madonna told him he could turn the cameras on at any moment and film her and her dancers and crew at any time, with one exception—no business meetings were to be shot. Madonna was taking a great chance allowing herself to be viewed not only in public, when she was in complete control, but also alone in her hotel room or goofing around with her dancers offstage. She even allowed Keshishian to film a throat examination she had at her New York apartment. Madonna's boyfriend Warren Beatty appears in the film, though he remains typically close-mouthed during most of his scenes, the main exception being the much-quoted line, "She doesn't want to *live* off-camera."

The film was groundbreaking in more ways than one. While Keshishian shot the performance sequences in full color, he did all the documentary, or "real-life" footage, in black and white. Keshishian captured many of Madonna's most personal moments on the tour. The camera follows Madonna as she visits her mother's grave during a stop in Detroit. Later, the audience sees an un-made-up Madonna, just out of bed, making business calls and dealing with paperwork. Keshishian also included many

Madonna stuns reporters by stripping off her dress during a press conference in May 1991 with Alek Keshishian (right), the director of her film *Truth or Dare,* at the Cannes Film Festival in France.

moments that show Madonna as the self-styled "mother" of her group. She takes the entire troupe shopping at Chanel in Paris, for example, and leads a group prayer before each show.

The color performance footage in *Truth or Dare* was as vibrant and immediate as the cinema-verité material. For the Blonde Ambition tour, Madonna performed new arrangements of many of the songs that had brought her celebrity. Several of these were featured in the film, including her startling performance of "Like a Virgin," during which she is flanked by two male dancers wearing conical appurtenances strapped to their chests. The complexly staged numbers also included a series of songs from *I'm Breathless,* during which she was joined by a chorus line of Dick Tracy look-alike dancers in long yellow raincoats.

Keshishian's film was a milestone for Madonna because it was an amazing real-life performance. In a 1991 interview with the *Advocate,* Madonna said "I told [Keshishian], 'You have to know that I'm going to want to throw you out of the room. You have to be willing to say no.'" He was, and his persistence was rewarded by the critics. *New York* magazine called *Truth or Dare* "a wonderful piece of work." *Rolling Stone* said it was "the most revealing and outrageously funny piece of pop demythologizing since D. A. Pennebaker blew the hype of Bob Dylan's 1965 English concert tour in *Don't Look Back.*"

In some ways, Madonna comes across unfavorably in the film: In one scene, she barks at concert technicians when problems arise; in another, when she is reunited with a childhood friend, Moira McPharlin, it is clear that Madonna's mind is elsewhere; and, after actor Kevin Costner tells her that her show was "neat," she turns to the camera and makes a gagging expression—not a subtle gesture in a film that would be seen by millions of people. Yet Madonna knew that showing the good with the bad

Madonna chats with her father, Tony, during a surprise reunion on the set of the "Arsenio Hall Show" in June 1992.

was part of the original plan. In fact, Madonna said that watching herself in the film was better than five years of psychoanalysis.

The Blonde Ambition tour sparked controversy all around the world. Because of some suggestive sequences, the Vatican asked that certain parts of the show be censored when it played in Rome, Italy. In Toronto, Canada, Madonna was told that if certain lurid movements were left in her concert she would be arrested after the show. Madonna did not change her show and was not arrested.

★ "YOU'RE A SUPERSTAR" ★

The stir Madonna's work caused was not lost on her critics in the media, nor on the academics. By the early 1990s, students at universities were studying Madonna's work in courses on American Pop Culture, Mass Media, and Women's Studies. Feminists were divided in their feelings about her outlandish behavior—one camp felt it was a battle cry of liberation and empowerment, while the other held the belief that Madonna was exploiting, not celebrating, her sex. In 1990, the controversial intellectual Camille Paglia joined the debate by writing, "Madonna is the true feminist." Paglia argued that, "Madonna has taught young women to be fully female and sexual while still exercising total control over their lives. She shows girls how to be attractive, sensual, energetic, ambitious, aggressive and funny—all at the same time." Psychologist Joyce Brothers, on the other hand, contended in *Entertainment Weekly* in 1992, "When you are a true feminist, you want power not for power's sake but you want to accomplish something. . . . I think it's kind of sad if young women use her as a role model."

After nearly a decade on the pop culture scene, the image of Madonna loomed as large as ever. She had conquered stage, screen, video, and radio, and she continued to hold a tight and steady rein on the public consciousness. She was an unparalleled master at gaining media attention. Each of her provocative new projects proved more scandalous than the last. The only question remaining was: How far would she go?

8 Deeper and Deeper

AFTER THE TRIUMPHANT CONCLUSION of her Blonde Ambition tour, which finished with an internationally broadcast performance seen by a record audience on cable television, Madonna focused her attention on other projects, including more films and a coffee-table book that tied in with a new album.

In 1991, moviegoers saw Madonna in Woody Allen's film *Shadows and Fog.* Madonna had a small role as a circus performer in the dreamlike, black-and-white film. Madonna was impressed by Allen's directing style. "I'll never learn patience," she said. "But I've learned, watching Woody, how a real artist works. Woody is a master of getting things out of people in a really gentle way. He's not a tyrant, and that's good for me to learn because I can be something of a tyrant in a working situation. Well, in a living situation, too."

Madonna next appeared in a supporting role in Penny Marshall's *A League of Their Own,* released at Christmas in 1992. The movie was about the all-woman baseball league that enjoyed a brief moment in the spotlight

Mimicking Marilyn Monroe, Madonna sings Stephen Sondheim's song "Sooner or Later," from the movie *Dick Tracy,* at the 1991 Academy Awards ceremony. Sondheim's composition won the Oscar for Best Original Song.

during World War II. The league, a sort of wartime novelty act, was created to fill the void left by American men who had been called for military duty. Critics gave the movie mostly favorable reviews, and it drew an impressive audience. The appraisals of Madonna's performance were generally neither very good nor very bad. However, more than one reviewer complained about the lack of range with which Madonna was expected to approach the role of a tough, gum-snapping, wisecracking city girl. Of Madonna's performance, David Denby wrote in *New York* magazine, "Marshall coldly uses

Willem Dafoe and Madonna costarred in the courtroom thriller *Body of Evidence* in 1992. Madonna played a character accused of killing an elderly man by inducing a heart attack with strenuous sex.

Madonna, who plays a slut and is treated like a slut. . . . To sell the movie with her name and then hardly give her a close-up is sheer cynicism."

Madonna's luck with Uli Edel's 1993 film *Body of Evidence,* in which she starred with Willem Dafoe, was even worse. In the picture, she plays a woman charged with murder for the death of an older man who suffers a heart attack while having sex with her. The critics dismissed the film on the whole, focusing especially on what they considered Madonna's poor performance. Critic Aris Cristofides said of Madonna's femme fatale in *Body*

of Evidence, "Not only is she a horrible actress, but she lacks the sort of easy, wicked sensuality of a Kathleen Turner or a Faye Dunaway—after all, sensuality stems from personality, not persona."

In October 1992, Madonna had unveiled another project, one that was unprecedented in the mainstream media and was easily her most daring artistic venture yet. For months, the public had been hearing and reading about a book Madonna was working on with photographer Steven Meisel. Madonna would write the text, and Meisel, who was known for his innovative fashion photography, would provide the pictures. Though it was a very personal project, the book was neither autobiography nor fiction but a strange combination of both. Madonna's latest feat was an actual book of erotica, based on her own personal sexual fantasies. Prior to the book's release, Madonna and Meisel arranged to keep the material top secret—no textual excerpts or photos were released as promotional material, and under no circumstances were pirated copies of photos or text permitted to circulate. The intense secrecy seemed designed both to protect the project from a curious and titillated public and to heighten her audience's interest and stimulation.

The book was bluntly titled *Sex.* Madonna did agree to speak about it in interviews before it hit the bookstores. The public learned that assorted actors, actresses, performers, and supermodels (including Isabella Rosellini, Vanilla Ice, and Naomi Campbell) had agreed to pose for what were sure to be controversial pictures. Other adventurous unknowns, chosen from a huge casting search, were also featured. Madonna divulged a series of incidents, each more uninhibited than the last, that occurred while shooting on location in Miami, Florida. In one instance, Madonna and her crew entered a local pizzeria, where Madonna ordered a slice of pizza. When her food arrived, Madonna shed her fur coat

(under which she was completely nude) and began to eat, with Meisel clicking away furiously. It was not long before the outraged owner of the pizzeria summoned the police, at which point Madonna and her crew quickly left. In a similar vein were pictures of Madonna pumping gas, wearing nothing but a pair of black lace leggings, and others of her hitchhiking naked.

Madonna's book of erotic photographs, *Sex,* raised more than a few eyebrows upon its release in 1992. The limited edition sold a million copies at $49.95.

Not all the material was so tongue-in-cheek, but Madonna was intent on conveying the humorous aspects of her book, which was a concerted attempt to demystify sex and sexual fantasies. "I don't have the same hang-ups that other people do, and that's the point I'm trying to make with this book," Madonna told *Vanity Fair*'s Maureen Orth in 1992. "I don't think that sex is bad. I don't think that nudity is bad. . . . I think the problem is that everybody's so uptight about it that they make it into something bad when it isn't."

The release of *Sex* was truly a national event. In bookstores from New York to San Francisco, people had

When Madonna adopted an Asian look for her video *Rain* in 1993, *Time* magazine opined, "She could be in the style vanguard again."

reserved copies weeks before the book actually arrived. On the first day of its release, U.S. stores sold 150,000 of the 500,000 copies printed for American distribution. Every copy of the one-time-only edition eventually was sold, despite its $49.95 price tag. The book came packaged in a Mylar bag to prevent peeking and to add to its mystique. The lavishly produced book had been designed by Fabien Baron, who had formerly been the art director of Andy Warhol's *Interview* magazine. Even the production of the book itself was unique—it was spiral-bound, notebook-style, and the cover was made of metal. As a bonus, each book came with a CD of "Erotica," the first single from Madonna's upcoming album, also titled *Erotica.*

Madonna's new book rekindled the debate sparked by her previous work. Critics and readers argued about whether it was a work of art or simply a publicity stunt that relied on its shock value rather than on any redeeming content. Many people also criticized it for not being erotic enough.

Madonna's *Erotica* album was scheduled for release in conjunction with her eyebrow- (and consciousness-) raising book. On October 2, 1992, MTV premiered the video for the title track, which featured footage from the photo shoots for the book. The network aired the clip at midnight, with an announcement that the video would only be shown in that time slot because of its explicit material.

The album was a collection of songs that ranged from smoky, pulsing dance tunes, like the title track and a remake of Peggy Lee's hit "Fever," to ballads like "Bad Girl" to "Deeper and Deeper," which, along with its accompanying video, was an homage to late-1970s disco tunes.

In the fall of 1993, Madonna costarred in director Abel Ferrara's film *Dangerous Game,* with Harvey Keitel and James Russo. In the movie, Madonna plays an actress who is cast in a film that explores domestic violence. Janet Maslin of the *New York Times* reviewed the picture on November 19, 1993, and said that Madonna's acting "is free of artifice in a way that Madonna's screen roles seldom are." Alex Patterson of the *New York Press* wrote, "Madonna, playing a bitchy prima donna, isn't exactly cast against type. . . . She has either learned how to act or finally found a character not so different from herself, whom she can simply *be* for the camera. In either case, she's terrific, exactly what the role requires."

During the last decade, Madonna has evolved from a material girl–boy toy to a mature, serious artist. She has tried her artistic hand at almost every medium and has mostly succeeded. There is no question that MTV had a great deal to do with exposing Madonna to the public and the media. Madonna not only helped popularize music videos, but turned them into an art form.

It might seem that Madonna's art, as well as her public persona, are solely concerned with controversy. Indeed, this is a driving force in her creative work, but she deals fearlessly with larger issues as well. Madonna has said, "I'm attracted to obstacles I need to overcome. I'm interested in facing challenges, things that are going to be harder rather than easier." As she once put it, "I'd rather walk through a fire than away from one."

Having lost many close friends to the AIDS epidemic, including artist Keith Haring and her early mentor Christopher Flynn (both died in 1990), Madonna has devoted much time and money to the cause of AIDS treatment and prevention. The Hollywood premiere of *Truth or Dare* was a benefit for AIDS Project Los Angeles. She is also a firm supporter of the gay rights movement, and in 1991 she received a media award from the Gay and Lesbian Alliance Against Defamation. She was a major backer for the Los Angeles production of John "Lypsynka" Epperson's *I Could Go on Lip-Synching!*, a drag show (performed by a man dressed as a woman) that has since been seen by audiences all around the country. She has appeared in fashion shows benefiting AIDS research, has been a vocal advocate of safe sex, and has used her art to bring non-heterosexual lifestyles into the mainstream. In this sense, she is a symbol of empowerment.

Her effect on the women's movement and the subsequent study of women's issues has been similar. Though people are often politically divided into pro- and anti-Madonna camps, there is no doubt that she has made an impact on how a whole generation of women view themselves. In addition to being a hardworking, prolific artist, Madonna is a shrewd and intelligent businesswoman. By April 1992, she owned not only her film production company, Siren, and several other related businesses, but a gigantic new venture with Warner Brothers as well. This newest brainchild is a multimedia, multimillion-dollar company called Maverick that includes its own record label. The new label is devoted to discovering promising new bands who work in a variety of musical styles. Her other thriving businesses include the irreverently named Boy Toy, Inc., and Slutco.

It is impossible to say what the next 10 years will bring for the woman who has become the pop queen of the past decade. It seems hard to believe that she will ever be anywhere other than in the public eye. Because of the sheer volume of work she has already produced, Madonna will surely remain a prevalent force in music and film. No doubt she will continue to evolve as an artist as well. As she wrote in "Like a Prayer," "Life is a mystery/Everyone must stand alone." Through her work, she has fearlessly probed life's mysteries and repeatedly challenged society's conventions and assumptions, daring her audiences to think, feel, and live freely. Standing alone and apart from others, she has forged a diverse and exhilarating career that has successfully merged the not-so-mainstream with the mainstream. As she said in 1990, "I feel that, as much as people complain and moan and groan and criticize me, they're affected by me. I've touched a nerve somehow." It is likely that—whatever else she accomplishes in the years to come—Madonna will continue to touch nerves.

Appendix ★ ★ ★ ★ ★ ★ ★ ★ ★ ★ ★ ★ ★ ★ ★ ★ ★

Filmography
(films and release dates)

A Certain Sacrifice, Commtron, 1985
(directed by Stephen Jon Lewicki)

Vision Quest, Warner Brothers, 1985
(directed by Harold Becker)

Desperately Seeking Susan, HBO,
1985 (directed by Susan
Seidelman)

Shanghai Surprise, Vestron, 1986
(directed by Jim Goddard)

Who's That Girl?, Warner Brothers,
1987 (directed by James Foley)

Bloodhounds of Broadway,
RCA/Columbia, 1989
(directed by Howard Brookner)

Dick Tracy, Touchstone, 1990
(directed by Warren Beatty)

Truth or Dare, Live Home Video,
1991 (directed by Alek Keshishian)

Shadows and Fog, Orion, 1992
(directed by Woody Allen)

A League of Their Own, Columbia,
1992 (directed by Penny Marshall)

Body of Evidence, MGM, 1993
(directed by Uli Edel)

Dangerous Game, MGM, 1993
(directed by Abel Ferrara)

Discography
(albums and release dates)

Madonna (7/83)

Like a Virgin (11/84)

True Blue (6/86)

You Can Dance (11/87)

Like a Prayer (3/89)

I'm Breathless (5/90)

The Immaculate Collection (11/90)

Erotica (10/92)

Home Videos
(with release dates)

Madonna (12/84)

Live—The Virgin Tour (11/85)

Ciao Italia—Live (5/88)

The Immaculate Collection (11/90)

Justify My Love (12/90)

Further Reading ★ ★ ★ ★ ★ ★ ★ ★ ★ ★ ★ ★ ★ ★ ★

Andersen, Christopher. *Madonna: Unauthorized.* New York: Island, 1991.

Bego, Mark. *Madonna: Blonde Ambition.* New York: Harmony Books, 1992.

Fisher, Carrie. "True Confessions: The Rolling Stone Interview with Madonna." Parts 1, 2. *Rolling Stone,* June 13 and 21, 1991.

Johnston, Becky. "Confessions of a Catholic Girl." *Interview,* May 1989, 54.

King, Norman. *Madonna: The Book.* New York: Morrow, 1991.

Petrow, Steven. "Madonna's Mad About the Boy." *The Advocate,* November 19, 1991, 86.

Sante, Luc. "Unlike a Virgin." *The New Republic,* August 20–27, 1990, 25.

Sexton, Adam, ed. *Desperately Seeking Madonna.* New York: Delta, 1993.

Shewey, Don. "Madonna: The Saint, The Slut, The Sensation . . ." *The Advocate,* May 7, 1991, 42.

———. "The Gospel According to Saint Madonna." *The Advocate,* May 21, 1991, 40.

Chronology ★ ★ ★ ★ ★ ★ ★ ★ ★ ★ ★ ★ ★ ★ ★ ★ ★

1958	Madonna Louise Ciccone is born on August 16 in Bay City, Michigan
1963	Madonna's mother, Madonna Fortin Ciccone, dies on December 1
1972	Enters Rochester Adams High School; enrolls at Christopher Flynn's Ballet School
1978	Arrives in New York City in July after dropping out of the University of Michigan, having completed only one year; studies modern dance with Pearl Lang
1980	Filming begins on *A Certain Sacrifice,* in which Madonna has her first acting role
1981	Forms a band, Emanon, with Steve Bray; signs first management contract with Adam Alter and Camille Barbone of Gotham Productions, which she breaks the following year
1982	Lands a contract with Warner Brothers Records
1983	*Madonna* album is released in July
1984	Performs "Like a Virgin" at the MTV Video Awards on September 14; *Like a Virgin* album released in November
1985	*Desperately Seeking Susan* released in March to rave reviews; embarks on Virgin tour; nude photos of Madonna appear in *Penthouse* and *Playboy;* performs at Live Aid; marries Sean Penn on August 16
1986	*True Blue* album is released in June; *Shanghai Surprise* is released in October and is panned by critics
1987	North American leg of Who's That Girl? tour begins; *Who's That Girl?* (film) is released
1988	David Mamet's play *Speed-the-Plow,* starring Madonna, opens on Broadway on April 6; Madonna appears with Sandra Bernhard on "Late Night with David Letterman"

1989   Files for divorce from Sean Penn; Pepsi announces a
       multimillion-dollar endorsement deal; *Like a Prayer* video
       debuts on MTV on March 3; Pepsi cancels Madonna ads;
       Like a Prayer album is released

1990   Appears as Breathless Mahoney in *Dick Tracy*;
       Blonde Ambition tour opens in Japan on May 13;
       performs "Vogue" at MTV Awards on September 4;
       video for "Justify My Love" is released in November;
       Madonna appears on ABC's "Nightline" to discuss
       controversy over her work

1991   Performs "Sooner or Later (I Always Get My Man)" from
       Dick Tracy at the Academy Awards on March 25; *Truth
       or Dare* premieres in May

1992   Forms Maverick productions, a subsidiary of Time/Warner;
       her book *Sex* is published in October; *Erotica* album is
       released; *A League of Their Own* premieres in December

1993   *Body of Evidence,* with Willem Dafoe, is released in January;
       Dangerous Game is relcased in November

Index ★

★ ★

Nicole Claro received her B.A. in literature from Bennington College. She currently lives in San Francisco, California, where she works as a production editor, studies capoeira (an Afro-Brazilian self-defense and dance form), and performs in dance, music, and theater pieces.

Leeza Gibbons is a reporter for and cohost of the nationally syndicated television program "Entertainment Tonight" and NBC's daily talk show "John & Leeza from Hollywood." A graduate of the University of South Carolina's School of Journalism, Gibbons joined the on-air staff of "Entertainment Tonight" in 1984 after cohosting WCBS-TV's "Two on the Town" in New York City. Prior to that, she cohosted "PM Magazine" on WFAA-TV in Dallas, Texas, and on KFDM-TV in Beaumont, Texas. Gibbons also hosts the annual "Miss Universe," "Miss U.S.A.," and "Miss Teen U.S.A." pageants, as well as the annual Hollywood Christmas Parade. She is active in a number of charities and has served as the national chairperson for the Spinal Muscular Atrophy Division of the Muscular Dystrophy Association; each September, Gibbons cohosts the National MDA Telethon with Jerry Lewis.

PICTURE CREDITS

Ron Akiyama/Star File, Inc.: p. 49; AP/Wide World Photos: pp. 10, 12–13, 20, 58, 64, 68–69, 83, 94, 99, 100–101, 110, 117; The Bettmann Archive: p. 36; Dance Collection, The New York Public Library for the Performing Arts at Lincoln Center: p. 32; Bob Gruen/Star File, Inc.: pp. 45, 72; Mark Harlan/Star File, Inc.: p. 16; Michigan Alumni Association Records, Box 137, Bentley Historical Library, University of Michigan: p. 34; Photofest: pp. 2, 61, 80, 114–15; Courtesy The Pontiac Public Library: p. 22; Chuck Pulin/Star File, Inc.: pp. 40, 54–55; Reuters/Bettmann: pp. 108, 112; Rochester Adams High School, 1973–1976, photo by Sharon Schwab: pp. 27, 28–29, 31; Star File, Inc.: p. 42; UPI/Bettmann: pp. 39, 75; © Warner Bros. Records: p. 118; Courtesy West Middle School, Rochester Hills, MI, photo by Sharon Schwab: p. 18; Vinnie Zuffante/Star File, Inc.: pp. 70, 85, 88, 90–91, 104.